The Battle for Open: How openness won and why it doesn't feel like victory

Martin Weller

]u[

ubiquity press
London

1007366210

Published by
Ubiquity Press Ltd.
Gordon House
29 Gordon Square
London WC1H 0PP
www.ubiquitypress.com

Text © Martin Weller 2014

First published 2014

Cover Image: ShutterStock

ISBN (Paperback): 978-1-909188-33-4
ISBN (EPUB): 978-1-909188-34-1
ISBN (PDF): 978-1-909188-35-8
ISBN (Kindle): 978-1-909188-36-5

DOI: http://dx.doi.org/10.5334/bam

Suggested citation:
Weller, M 2014 *The Battle For Open: How openness won and why
it doesn't feel like victory.* London: Ubiquity Press. DOI: http://
dx.doi.org/10.5334/bam

To read the free, open access version of this book
online, visit http://dx.doi.org/10.5334/bam
or scan this QR code with your mobile device:

Author details

Martin Weller

The Open University

Martin Weller is Professor of Educational Technology at the Open University in the UK. He chaired the OU's first major elearning course in 1999, with over 12,000 students, and has led several major elearning initiatives. He started blogging in 2005 and became interested in the impact of new technology on academic practice. He is currently the Director of the OER Research Hub project and holds the ICDE Chair in OER.

To three pioneers of modern open education:
Stephen Downes, George Siemens and David Wiley

Contents

Acknowledgements

The discussions around openness in its various forms take place in many different forums and with people who have different priorities. The following have been particularly influential in shaping my thoughts in this area, in providing feedback on blog posts and engaging in conversation both online and face to face.

At the Open University, the OER Research Hub team have provided much of the basis for this work, so my thanks go to Patrick McAndrew, Rob Farrow, Leigh-Anne Perryman, Bea de os Arcos, Beck Pitt, Claire Walker, Simone Arthur, Natalie Eggleston, Gary Elliott-Cirigottis and Martin Hawksey.

Those in the UK who have been influential in many of the arguments in this book include David Kernohan, Sheila MacNeill, Richard Hall, Josie Fraser, Joss Winn, Doug Clow, Katy Jordan and Cristina Costa.

I am fortunate to have a global network of peers and friends who regularly leave me feeling inadequate with the insight they bring to many topics; these include Audrey Watters, Brian Lamb, Jim Groom, Bonnie Stewart, Dave Cormier, Laura Pasquini, George Veletsianos, Michael Feldstein, Phil Hill, Valerie Irvine, Mike Caulfield, Cable Green, Alan Levine, Catherine Cronin, Alec Couros and Wayne Mackintosh.

This book draws on much of the work of the OER Research Hub which was funded through the generous support of the William and Flora Hewlett Foundation, and I would like to offer my thanks to them, in particular Kathy Nicholson, TJ Bliss and Barbara Chow. The opinions expressed herein are my own, however, and should not be interpreted as the views of any particular organisation.

CHAPTER 1

The Victory of Openness

It made me think that everything was about to arrive - the
moment when you know all and everything is decided forever.
—Jack Kerouac

Introduction

Openness is everywhere in education at the moment: in late 2011 a free course in artificial intelligence had over 160,000 learners enrolled (Leckart 2012); in 2012 in the UK the Government followed other national bodies in the US and Canada by announcing a policy mandating that all articles resulting from publicly funded research should be made freely available in open access publications (Finch Group 2012); downloads from Apple's iTunes U site, which gives away free educational content, passed 1 billion in 2013 (Robertson 2013); British Columbia announced a policy in 2012 to provide open, free textbooks for the 40 most popular courses (Gilmore 2012); the G8 leaders signed a treaty on open data in June 2013, stating that all government data will be released openly by default (UK Cabinet Office 2013). Outside of these headline figures there are fundamental shifts in practices: academics are creating and releasing their own content using tools such as Slideshare and YouTube; researchers are releasing results earlier and using open, crowdsourcing approaches; every day millions of people make use of free, open online tools and resources to learn and share.

In fact, openness is now such a part of everyday life that it seems unworthy of comment. This wasn't always the case, nor did it appear inevitable or predictable. At the end of the '90s, as the dot-com boom was gaining pace, there was plenty of scepticism around business models (much of it justified after the collapse) and similarly with the web 2.0 bubble ten years later. And while many of the business models were unsustainable, the traditional models of paying for content have also been shown not to map across to the new digital domain. 'Giving stuff away' is no longer an approach to be mocked.

Nowhere has openness played such a central role as in education. Many of the pioneers of open movements have come from universities. The core functions of academics are all subject to radical change under an open model; from the Massive Open Online Courses (MOOCs) that are challenging teaching to pre-publication repositories that undermine the traditional publishing and review model of researchers, openness affects all aspects of higher education.

Openness has a long history in higher education. Its foundations lie in one of altruism and the belief that education is a public good. It has undergone many interpretations and adaptations, moving from a model which had open entry to study as its primary focus to one that emphasises openly available content and resources. This change has largely been a result of the digital and network revolution. Changes in other sectors, most notably the open source model of software production and values associated with the internet of free access, and open approaches have influenced (and been influenced by) practitioners in higher education. The past decade or so has seen the growth of a global open education movement, with significant funding from bodies such as the William and Flora Hewlett Foundation and research councils. Active campaigners in universities have sought to establish programmes that will release content – including data, teaching resources and publications – openly; others have adopted open practices through social media and blogs. This has been combined with related work on open licences, most notably that of Creative Commons, which allow easy reuse and adaptation of content, advocacy at policy level for nation- or state-wide adoption of open content and sharing of resources, and improved technology and infrastructure that make this openness both easy and inexpensive.

One might therefore expect this to be a time of celebration for the advocates of openness. Having fought so long for their message to be heard, they are now being actively courted by senior management for their experience and views on various open strategies. Open approaches are featured in the mainstream media. Millions of people are enhancing their learning through open resources and open courses. Put bluntly, it looks as though openness has won. And yet you would be hard pushed to find any signs of celebration amongst those original advocates. They are despondent about the reinterpretation of openness to mean 'free' or 'online' without some of the reuse liberties they had envisaged. Concerns are expressed about the commercial interests that are now using openness as a marketing tool. Doubts are raised regarding the benefits of some open models for developing nations or learners who require support. At this very moment of victory it seems that the narrative around openness is being usurped by others, and the consequences of this may not be very open at all.

In 2012 Gardner Campbell gave a keynote presentation at the Open Education conference (Campbell 2012) in which he outlined these concerns and frustrations. 'What we are seeing,' he said, 'are developments in the higher education landscape that seem to meet every one of the criteria we have set forth for open education – increased access, decreased cost, things that will allow more people than ever on a planetary scale, one billion individual learners at a time … Isn't that what we meant?' But as he explored different successes of openness his refrain was that of T. S. Eliot: that's not what I meant at all.

Why should this be the case? Can we dismiss it as just sour grapes? Are the advocates of openness merely exhibiting chagrin that others are now claiming openness? Is it just a semantic argument over interpretation that has little interest beyond a few academics? Or is it something more fundamental, regarding the direction of openness and the ways it is implemented? It is this central tension in openness, that of victory and simultaneous anxiety, that this book seeks to explore.

Higher Education and Openness

The focus of this book is primarily on higher education. The justification for this focus is that it is the area where the battle for open is perhaps most keenly contested. However, open education can be viewed as only one component of a broader open movement. There is an active open data community, which seeks to make data – particularly governmental and corporation data – openly available. Organisations such as the Open Knowledge Foundation see access to data as fundamental in accountability and engagement across a range of social functions, including politics, retail, energy, health, etc. This places openness as activism, of which education is only one aspect. As the Open Knowledge Foundation states, 'We want to see open knowledge being a mainstream concept, and as natural and important to our everyday lives and organisations as green is today' (OKFN n.d).

The focus on education allows the battle for open to be explored in detail across four examples, although many of these intersect with the wider open movement, such as open access to published articles and the release of research data. Unlike some sectors which have had openness rather foisted upon them as a result of the digital revolution – for example, the music industry and the arrival of sharing services such as Napster – higher education has sought to develop open practices in a range of areas.

It is this scope that makes it such a vibrant area of study, encompassing publishing, teaching, technology, individual practices, broadcast and engagement. There is much that is relevant for other sectors here also, where one or more of these topics will be applicable, but rarely the entire range. It is frequently stated that higher education can learn lessons from other sectors that have been impacted by the digital revolution, such as newspapers, but the opposite may be true with regards to openness; other sectors can learn much from what is played out in the openness debate in higher education.

What are the key areas of interest, then, with regards to openness and higher education? Each of these will be explored in a chapter of their own, but the main developments are summarised below.

Teaching

The advent of MOOCs has garnered a lot of attention recently. Originally developed as an experimental method of exploring the possibilities of networked learning, MOOCs became the subject of media and commercial interest following the large numbers attracted to Sebastian Thrun's Artificial Intelligence MOOC. Since then the major commercial player to emerge is Coursera, with two rounds of venture capital funding and over 4 million learners registered on its 400 courses (Coursera 2013a).

The idea behind MOOCs is simple: make online courses open to anyone and remove the costly human support factor. Whether this model is financially sustainable is still open to question as it is in the early stages. But there has been no shortage of media attention and discussion, with some observers arguing that MOOCs are the internet's effect on higher education.

MOOCs are just one aspect of how openness is influencing the teaching function of higher education, however. Before MOOCs there was (and still is) the successful Open Educational Resources (OER) movement. It began in 2001 when the Hewlett foundation funded MIT to start the OpenCourseWare site, which released lecture material freely. Since then, the OER movement has spread globally. There are now major initiatives in all continents, and OER has formed part of the central strategy for many education programmes, including UNESCO, the Shuttleworth Foundation, the William and Flora Hewlett foundation and the Higher Education Funding Council for England (HEFCE). The distinction between MOOCs and OERs may be blurring somewhat – for example, if a set of OER resources are packaged into a course structure, does that make them a MOOC? Similarly, if a MOOC is made available after the course has finished, is it then an OER? Related to OERs is the move to establish open textbooks, with the cost of textbooks particularly in the US becoming a prohibitive factor in higher education participation. Open textbooks seek to replace these publisher-owned versions of standard, introductory texts with free, open online versions that have been created by groups or single authors. This is having significant impact; for example, the open textbook initiative OpenStax aims to provide free online and low-cost print textbooks to 10 million students, and currently has over 200 colleges signed up, with projected savings to students of US$90 million over the next five years (OpenStax 2013).

Research

Open access publishing has been growing steadily in acceptance as not only a valid, but rather the best model of disseminating research publications. Instead of academics publishing in proprietary journals, access to which is then purchased by libraries or on article basis by individuals, open access makes publications freely accessible to all. There are different models for achieving this: the so-called Green route, whereby the author places the article on their own site or the institutions repository; the Gold route, where the publisher charges a fee to make the article openly available; and the Platinum route, where the journal operates for free.

Open access publishing is perhaps the most recognisable aspect of how scholarly activity is adapting to the opportunities afforded by digital and networked technology. Other practices form what is termed open scholarship and include sharing individual resources such as presentations, podcasts and bibliographies; social media engagement through blogs, twitter and other routes; and generally more open practices, such as pre-publishing book chapters, open reviews and open research methods. The latter can include the use of approaches such as crowdsourcing and social media analysis, which rely on openness to succeed. Open scholarship is also providing new avenues for public engagement as academics create online identities that previously would have necessitated a broadcast intermediary to establish.

One aspect of open scholarship is that of open data, making the data from research projects publicly available (where it is not sensitive). As mentioned at the start of this chapter, the G8 have signed an agreement that this should be the default position on governmental data, and many research funders impose similar constraints. For many subjects, such as climate change, this allows for larger data sets to be created and meta-studies to be conducted, improving the overall quality of the analysis. In other subjects too it provides the possibility of comparisons, analysis and interpretations that are unpredictable and may be outside of the original domain.

Open Policy

Much of the work around open licensing, particularly that of Creative Commons, has been initiated in or influenced by higher education. Licensing is, in the eyes of many, one of the true tests of openness, as the ability to take and reuse an artefact is what differentiates open from merely free. Licences are the main route through which broader policy based initiatives can be realised. By adopting a position on licences, governments, charities, research funders, publishers and technology companies create a context whereby openness follows. The promotion of openness then as an approach, both practical and ethical, has been a growing strand of the open movement based in higher education.

This brief overview should attest that openness lies at the heart of much of the change in higher education, and that there is a significant amount of research and activity in this area. One aim of this book is to highlight and even celebrate this activity. It is an exciting time to be involved in higher education; there are opportunities for changing practice in nearly all aspects, and openness is the key to many of these. Succeeding in this, however, requires firstly engaging with the changes, and secondly taking ownership of the changes and not allowing them to be dictated by external forces, either through vacillation or a short-term desire to simplify matters. Below we shall consider analogy with the green movement, which demonstrates that the value of openness will not be lost on others.

Why Openness Matters

In the preceding sections I hope I have started to convince you that openness has been largely victorious as an approach. By victorious I do not necessarily mean that all academics and students have it at the forefront of their minds, but one aspect of open education or another touches upon the practice of both learners and academics, be it students using open resources to supplement their learning, or academics publishing open access journals. There is undoubtedly still a lot more that open education needs to do before it affects all aspects of practice, but the current period marks the moment when open education stopped being a peripheral, specialist interest and began to occupy a place in the mainstream of academic practice. If you are still unconvinced, then this will be explored further in chapters 3 to 7. I now want to set out an argument regarding its significance and why you should care about the arguments around openness. There are two main reasons that openness in education matters: opportunities and function.

Under 'opportunities' there are many sub-categories that can be listed, but I will focus on just one example here, as other opportunities are explored throughout the book. One significant opportunity that openness affords is in the area of pedagogy. In *The Digital Scholar* (Weller 2011) I set out how digital resources and the internet are causing a shift from a pedagogy of scarcity to one of abundance. Many of our existing teaching models (the lecture is a good example) are based around the starting assumption of access to knowledge being scarce (hence we gather lots of people in a room to hear an expert speak). Abundant online content changes this assumption. A pedagogy of abundance focuses on content, however, which is an important, but not sole element in the overall approach. Perhaps it is better to talk of a pedagogy of openness. Open pedagogy makes use of open content, such as open educational resources, videos, podcasts, etc., but also places an emphasis on the network and the learner's connections within this. In analysing the pedagogy of MOOCs (although open pedagogy is not confined to MOOCs), Paul Stacey (2013) makes the following recommendations:

- Be as open as possible. Go beyond open enrolments and use open pedagogies that leverage the entire web, not just the specific content in the MOOC platform. As part of your open pedagogy strategy use OER and openly license your resources using Creative Commons licenses in a way that allows reuse, revision, remix, and redistribution. Make your MOOC platform open source software. Publish the learning analytics data you collect as open data using a CC0 license.
- Use tried and proven modern online learning pedagogies, not campus classroom based didactic learning pedagogies which we know are ill-suited to online learning.
- Use peer-to-peer pedagogies over self-study. We know this improves learning outcomes. The cost of enabling a network of peers is the same as that of networking content – essentially zero.

- Use social learning, including blogs, chat, discussion forums, wikis, and group assignments.
- Leverage massive participation – have all students contribute something that adds to or improves the course overall.

Examples of open pedagogy would include Jim Groom's DS106, an open course which encourages learners to create daily artefacts, suggest assignments, establish their own space online and be part of a community that extends beyond the course both geographically and temporally. Dave Cormier starts his educational technology course every year by asking students to create a contract stating 'that each of you decide how much work you would like to do for what grade. Individual assignments are given a "satisfactory" or "unsatisfactory" assessment upon completion' (Cormier 2013). Courses such as Octel (http://octel.alt.ac.uk) have learners create their own blogs, and this is used for all their solutions. The course then automatically aggregates all of these contributions into one central blog. All of this is conducted in the open.

This is not to suggest that any of these examples should be the default or adopted by others. They are suited to particular contexts and topics. The point is a more general one, in that openness is a philosophical cornerstone in these courses. It is present in the technology adopted, in the resources referenced, in the activities students undertake and in the teaching approaches taken. All of this is made possible by openness in several other areas: resources need to be made openly available, technology needs to be free to use, students need to be prepared to work in the open and universities need to accept these new models of operating. I would suggest that we are only just at the beginning of exploring models of teaching and learning that have this open mindset. It is notable that many of these early experimenters in open pedagogy are people associated with the open education movement. One could argue that they have been infected by the open mindset and seek to explore its possibilities whenever they can.

It is this opportunity to explore that is important for higher education if it is to innovate and make best use of the possibilities that openness offers. A prerequisite for this is engagement with open education, whether it is in terms of technology, resources or pedagogy. One of the dangers of outsourcing openness, for example, by relying on third-party vendors to provide MOOC platforms or relying on publishers to provide open content, is that the scope for experimentation becomes limited. The pre-packaged solution becomes not just the accepted method, but the *only* method which is recognised.

We are already seeing some of this; for example, Georgia Tech announced a collaboration with MOOC company Udacity to offer an online Master's degree. As Christopher Newfield (2103) notes in an analysis of the contract, Udacity has an exclusive relationship, so Georgia Tech cannot offer its own content elsewhere. Udacity can, however, offer that content to other learners outside of the program. Newfield argues that, as they seek to recoup costs, 'the big savings, ironically, come by squeezing innovation – payments to course creators flatten out – and by leveraging overhead'.

Even if we accept a less cynical view of this arrangement, the model of companies such as Udacity, Coursera and Pearson is to create a global brand by becoming one of only a handful of providers. Diversity in the market is not in their interest, and so the model of how to create MOOCs or deliver online resources becomes restricted, whether by contractual arrangements or simply by the presence of pre-packaged solutions which negate further exploration.

This same message regarding the possibility for experimentation can be repeated for nearly all other university functions: research, public engagement or the creation of resources. In each area the possibilities of combining open elements and making use of the digital networked environment allow for new opportunities, but in order to be fully realised these require active engagement and innovation by higher education institutions and academics, rather than external provision.

This brings us onto the second reason why openness matters, namely the function, or role, of the university. Universities can be seen as a bundle of different functions: research, teaching, public engagement, policy guidance and incubators for ideas and businesses. In times of financial downturn, every aspect of society is examined for its contribution versus its cost, and the higher education sector is no exception. Increasingly, the narrative is one of a straightforward investment transaction – students pay a certain fee, and in return they receive an education that will allow them to earn more money later in life (e.g. Buchanan 2013).

While this is certainly a defensible and logical perspective for many to take, it ignores or downplays other contributions. Open approaches to the dissemination of research, sharing of teaching resources and online access to conferences and seminars helps to reinforce the broader role of the university. There is nothing particularly new in this; my own institution, The Open University (OU), is well regarded in the UK even by those who have never studied there, largely as a result of their collaboration with the BBC in making educational programmes. These can be seen as early forms of open educational resources. However, the OU's relationship with the national broadcaster puts it in a privileged position. Open approaches allow all institutions to adopt some of this approach, often at relatively low cost. For example, the

University of Glamorgan (now University of South Wales) set up its own iTunesU site in 2010 at relatively low cost and generated over 1 million downloads in the first 18 months (Richards 2010).

Increasingly, then, we can see that openness helps shape the identity not just of a particular university, but of higher education in general and its relationship to society.

I will end with one small example, which pulls together many of the strands of openness. Katy Jordan is a PhD student at the OU focusing on academic networks on sites such as Academia. edu. She has studied a number of MOOCs on her own initiative to supplement the formal research training offered at the University. One of these was an infographics MOOC offered by the University of Texas. For her final visualisation project on this open course she decided to plot MOOC completion rates on an interactive graph, and blogged her results (Jordan 2013). This was picked up by a prominent blogger, who wrote about it being the first real attempt to collect and compile completion data for MOOCs (Hill 2013), and he also tweeted it.

MOOC completion rates are a subject of much interest, and so Katy's post went viral, and became the de-facto piece to link to on completion rates, which almost every MOOC piece references. It led to further funding through the MOOC Research Initiative and publications. All on the back of a blog post.

This small example illustrates how openness in different forms spreads out and has unexpected impact. The course needed to be open for Katy to take it; she was at liberty to share her results and did so as part of her general, open practice. The infographic and blog relies on open software and draws on openly available data that people have shared about MOOC completions, and the format of her work means others can interrogate that data and suggest new data points. The open network then spreads the message because it is open access and can be linked to and read by all.

It's hard to predict or trigger these events, but a closed approach anywhere along the chain would have prevented it. It is in the replication of small examples like this across higher education that the real value of openness lies.

Is It a Battle?

Having hopefully gone some way to convincing you of the victory of openness and why the future direction of openness is significant, I now want to set out why I have used the term 'battle' and view it is a time of conflict. I know some readers will be uncomfortable with such militaristic language, but its use is deliberate in highlighting some of the significant factors about openness.

Firstly, there is a real conflict at the heart of the direction openness takes. We'll explore this more throughout this book, but for many of the proponents of openness its key attribute is about freedom – for individuals to access content, to reuse it in ways they see fit, to develop new methods of working and to take advantage of the opportunities the digital, networked world offers. The more commercial interpretation of openness may see it as an initial tactic to gain users on a proprietary platform, or as a means of accessing government funding. Some see the new providers as entirely usurping existing providers in higher education, such as when Sebastian Thrun predicts there will be only ten global providers of education in the future (and he hopes his company, Udacity, is one of them) (*The Economist* 2012)

This is not a polite debate about definitions then; there will be very real consequences for education and society in general about who wins in the battle for openness. This highlights the second factor in choosing the term, namely that, like in real battles, things of value are being fought over. The average cumulative expenditure per student in OECD (Organisation for Economic Co-operation and Development) countries for tertiary studies is US$57,774 (OECD 2013), and the global education market has been estimated to be worth US$5–6 trillion (Shapiro 2013). In academic publishing Reed Elsevier reported revenue of over £6 billion in 2012, of which over 2 billion was for the Science, Technical and Medical publishing field (Reed Elsevier 2012) while Springer reported sales of €875 million in 2011 (Springer 2011). These are big markets, and the demand for education is not going to disappear, so they represent highly desirable ones in times of global recession.

My third, and final, justification for using the term 'battle', is that, as well as the very considerable spoils that may go to the victor, the phrase about the victors writing history is also pertinent. There is a battle for narrative taking place which circles around the issues of openness. An example of this is explored in Chapter 6, where we look at the recurrent 'education is broken' meme and the related Silicon Valley narrative for education. These both seek to place higher education as a simple content industry, akin to the music business, and therefore can provide a simple, technological solution to this supposedly broken system. These narratives are often accepted unchallenged and deliberately ignore higher education's role in many of the changes that have occurred (positioning it as external forces fixing higher education) or simplifying the functions of higher education.

The term 'battle' then seems appropriate to convey these three themes of conflict, value and narrative. After the initial victory of openness, we are now entering the key stage in the longer-term battle around openness. And this is not simply about whether we use one piece of technology or another; openness is at the very heart of higher education in the 21st century. In its most positive interpretation, it is the means by which higher education becomes more relevant to society by opening up its knowledge and access to its services. It provides the means by which higher education adapts to the changed context of the digital world. At its most pessimistic, openness is the route by which commerce fundamentally undermines the higher education system to the point where it is weakened beyond repair. I hope to make the case through this book that the battle for open can be viewed more significantly as a battle for the future of education.

Lessons from Elsewhere

We can begin to see why the celebrations regarding the victory of openness are muted by way of two brief analogies. The first is that of nearly all revolutions and their immediate aftermath. The French Revolution of 1789 saw an undeniable positive movement to overthrow injustices imposed by a monarchy. In the subsequent decade there were numerous struggles between factions, a dictatorship and the Reign of Terror, culminating in the rise of Napoleon. Although the long-term results of the revolution were positive, during the decade and more after the 1789 commencement, it must have felt very different for the average French citizen. During the rule of Robespierre and the Jacobins it may not have been clear whether it was in fact better under the old regime. One hears similar observations after more recent revolutions – for instance, Russians proclaiming that life was better under Stalin or East Germans that they preferred the communist regime (Bonstein 2009). A more recent example is the Arab Spring, which after two years has left many countries facing division, worsening economic performance and continued violent struggle.

Many of the participants in a post-revolutionary state would be unified by one thought: *this isn't what victory should feel like*. The interests of various groups can come into the uncertainty revolution creates, the old power structures do not disappear quietly, the pressures of everyday concerns lead to infighting amongst previous allies, and so on. It is messy, complex and all very human.

One interpretation of these national revolutions is that these post-revolutionary struggles are the inevitable growing pains of a democracy but the general direction is towards greater freedom. Viewed from an historical perspective they can seem entirely predictable given the sudden nature of change. And this also provides a second, more general lesson – it is after the initial victory, in these periods of change, that the real shape of the long-term goal is determined.

A second analogy is provided by the green movement. Once seen as peripheral and only of concern to hippies, the broad green message has moved into central society. Products are advertised as being green, recycling is widely practised, alternative energy sources are part of a national energy plan and all major political parties are urged to have green policies. The environmental impact of any major planning decision is now high on the agenda, even if it isn't always the priority. From the perspective of the 1950s, this looks like radical progress, a victory of the green message. And yet for many in the green movement, it doesn't feel like victory at all. The ongoing global struggle to put into place meaningful agreements on carbon emissions and the complex politics involved in getting agreement on global, long-term interests from local, short-term politicians have made the green message a victim of its own success. It has penetrated so successfully into the mainstream that it is now a marketable quality. This is necessary to have an impact at the individual level, for example in consideration of purchasing choices regarding cars, light-bulbs, food, clothing, travel, etc. But it has also been co-opted by companies who see it as a means of marketing a product. For example, many green activists in the 1970s would not have predicted that nuclear power would find renewed interest by promoting its green (carbon dioxide free) credentials. Regardless of what you feel about nuclear power, we can probably assume that raising its profile was not high on the list of hoped-for outcomes for many green activists.

In 2010, assets in the US where environmental performance was a major component were valued at US$30.7 trillion, compared with US$639 billion in 1995 (Delmas & Burbano 2011). Being green is definitely part of big business. This leads to companies labelling products as green on a rather spurious basis. Like 'fat-free' or 'diet' in food labelling, 'eco-friendly', 'natural' or 'green' are labels that often hide other sins or are dubious in their claim. This is termed greenwashing, for example, the Airbus A380 reportedly has 17% less carbon emissions than a Boeing 747, which is to be welcomed, but adverts promoting it as an environmentally friendly option would seem to be stretching the definition somewhat. Similarly BP's series of 'green' adverts aimed at promoting a 'beyond petroleum' message provide a good example of how the green message can be adopted by companies who would seem to be fundamentally at odds with it.

Environmental marketing agency Terra Choice, identified '7 sins of greenwashing' (Terra Choice 2010), analogies of which we will see in the open world, so it's worth listing them here:

1) Sin of the Hidden Trade-off – whereby an unreasonably narrow set of attributes is used to claim greenness, without attention to other important environmental issues.

2) Sin of No Proof – when an environmental claim cannot be substantiated by easily accessible supporting information.

3) Sin of Vagueness – making poorly defined or broad claims so that their real meaning is likely to be misunderstood by the consumer.

4) Sin of Irrelevance – a claim that is truthful but is unimportant or unhelpful.

5) Sin of Lesser of Two Evils – making claims that may be true within the product category, but that risk distracting the consumer from the greater environmental impacts of the category as a whole.

6) Sin of Fibbing – making wholly false claims.

7) Sin of Worshiping False Labels – when a product, through either words or images, gives the impression of third-party endorsement where no such endorsement actually exists.

In the IT world the similarities between greenwashing and claims to openness have led to the term 'openwashing' being used. Klint Finley explains (2011):

> The old 'open vs. proprietary' debate is over and open won. As IT infrastructure moves to the cloud, openness is not just a priority for source code but for standards and APIs as well. Almost every vendor in the IT market now wants to position its products as 'open.' Vendors that don't have an open source product instead emphasize having a product that uses 'open standards' or has an 'open API.'

As companies adopt open credentials in education we are seeing the term applied in that sphere too, with similar cynicism (Wiley 2011a). Like 'green', there are a series of positive connotations associated with the term 'open' – after all, who would argue for being closed? The commercial co-option of green then provides us with a third lesson to be applied to the open movement: the definition of the term will be turned to commercial advantage. We will see this openwashing in later examples in the book, particularly with regards to MOOCs.

These two analogies provide us with three lessons then that will be seen repeatedly as different areas of open education are examined. My interpretation of what these analogies offer us is as follows:

1) Victory is more complex than first envisaged.
2) The future direction is shaped by the more prosaic struggles that come after initial victory.
3) Once a term gains mainstream acceptance it will be used for commercial advantage.

If we consider these with regards to open education, then it's hard not to conclude that openness has prevailed. The victory may not be absolute, but the trend is in that direction – it seems unlikely that we will return to closed systems in academia anymore than we will return to Encyclopaedia Britannica salesmen knocking on doors. Whether it's open access publishing, open data, MOOCs, OERs, open source or open scholarship, the openness message has been accepted as a valid approach (which is not to say it should be the only approach).

Time to rejoice, one might think, but, of course, as the first lesson shows us, it's never that simple. When it was simply open vs. closed there was a clear distinction: Openness was good, closed was bad. As the victory bells sound, though, it doesn't take much examination to reveal that it has become a more complex picture. This is the nature of victory.

So it is with openness – we shouldn't view this as an opportunity missed or romanticise some brief period when there was a brief openness Camelot, now despoiled. The general direction is positive, but with this comes increased complexity. The second lesson highlights this: we replace open vs. closed with a set of more complex, nuanced debates, which may seem rather specialised. For example:

- different approaches to MOOC pedagogy, so called xMOOCs vs. cMOOCs (we will address these in chapter 5)
- different licences, such as the more open Creative Commons CC-BY licence vs. the CC-NC one which restricts commercial use
- different routes to open access, the Gold vs. Green debate
- different technology options, for example centralised MOOC platforms vs. a distributed mix of third-party services

It is from these smaller debates that the larger picture is formed, and it is the construction of this larger picture that the remainder of this book will seek to perform.

Conclusions

The nature of the victory of openness and subsequent struggle can be illustrated with an example where the battle around openness is perhaps most advanced, namely, open access publishing. This is explored in more detail in Chapter 3, but a shortened version here can be used to illustrate the broader argument of this chapter.

The conventional model of academic publishing has usually seen academics providing, reviewing and often editing papers for free, which are published by commercial publishers and access to which is sold to libraries in bundles. Much of the funding for the research that informs these articles and the time spent on producing them comes from public funds, so over the last decade there has been a demand to make them publicly accessible. This has now become the mandate for many research funders, and many governments have adopted open access policies at a national level which stipulate that the findings of publicly funded research are made publicly available. This has extended to data from research projects as well as publications. Open access publishing is now the norm for many academics, and not just those who might be deemed early adopters; a survey by Wiley of its authors found that 59% had published in open access journals (Warne, 2013).

In the UK the 2012 Finch report (Finch Group 2012) recommended that 'a clear policy direction should be set towards support for publication in open access or hybrid journals, funded by APCs, as the main vehicle for the publication of research, especially when it is publicly funded'. APCs are Article Process Charges; this is often termed the Gold route to open access, whereby authors (or more often the research funders) pay the publishers for an article to be made open access. This is in contrast with the Green route, where it is self-archived, or the Platinum route, which are journals where there is no APC charge.

In this we can see the initial triumph of openness. Open access has moved from the periphery to the mainstream and become the recommended route for publishing research articles. But at the same time, the conflicts around implementation are also evident, as is the thwarting of the original open ambitions.

The Finch report has been criticised for seeking to protect the interests of commercial publishers, while not encouraging alternative methods such as Green or Platinum open access (Harnad 2012). In addition, the pay-to-publish model has seen the rise of a number of dubious open access journals, which seek to use openwashing as a means to make profit while ignoring the quality of articles. Bohannon (2013) reports on a fake article that was accepted by 157 open access journals. This would indicate that the pay-to-publish model creates a different stress on the filter to publish.

The tensions in the open access publishing world are representative of those in all aspects of openness in education: Incumbents have a vested interest in maintaining the status quo; there are considerable sums of money involved; the open approach allows new entrants to the market; the open label becomes a marketing tool; and there are tensions in maintaining the best aspects of existing practice as we transition to new ones. Driving it all is a conviction that the open model is the best approach, both in terms of access and innovation. The Public Library of Science (PLoS), for instance, has not only interpreted open access to mean free access to content, but also used the open approach to rethink the process of peer review and the type of articles they publish, such as the PLoS Currents, which provide rapid peer-review around focused topics (http://currents.plos.org/)

About This Book

This book is aimed primarily at those working in higher education who have an interest in open education. It does not assume specialist knowledge of open education or educational technology. The aim of the book is to set out the manner in which openness has been successful as an approach, but more significantly to reveal the tensions in each area. By the end of the book I hope to have convinced you that the future direction of openness is relevant to all those in higher education.

Chapter 2 explores the nature of openness in education in more detail and, in particular, the significant influences that have shaped it. The next five chapters then examine the higher education response to openness in four key areas, namely open access publishing, open educational resources, MOOCs and open scholarship. As the battle for narrative is best exemplified by MOOCs, Chapter 6 takes a brief detour to consider this. In each of these chapters the aims of the book will be examined further. Firstly, the story of success of openness in that area will be set out. This book is as much a celebration of the open education movement as it is a critique of the current tensions. Then the key areas of tension, the battlegrounds, are discussed. Lastly, future directions proposed. In this manner I hope to reiterate the themes of the victory of openness, its significance and the tensions that have been highlighted in this chapter. Chapter 8 takes a more critical appraisal of the issues around openness, and Chapter 9 proposes resilience as an alternative narrative for considering change in higher education. Finally, in Chapter 10, some means of framing the future direction of open education are proposed.

•

CHAPTER 2

What Sort of Open?

What if in fact there were ever only like two really distinct individual people walking around back there in history's mist? That all difference descends from this difference?

—David Foster Wallace

Introduction

Having outlined the broad argument of the book in the previous chapter, this chapter will add some depth to the concept of 'open' as it relates to education, setting out motivations for the open approach, and some of the relevant history in the development of open education. This will help inform the next five chapters, each of which takes a particular example of open education.

In the previous chapter the acceptance of the open approach in education was set forward. One needs only consider the variety of ways in which the term 'open' has been used as a prefix to note this: open courses, open pedagogy, open educational resources, open access, open data, open scholarship – it seems every aspect of educational practice is subject to being 'open' now. I work at the Open University in the UK and often comment that if you were establishing a university now, then 'Open University' would be a good choice of name. It has certainly aged better than some of the alternatives that were suggested at its inception, including 'the University of the Air'.

The examples of openness mentioned can be seen as the latest interpretations of that approach as applied to education. But these forms of openness did not arise in a vacuum, and their roots have more than just a historical interest for the current debates. In this chapter I will explore some of the history of openness in education in order to establish a basis for the subsequent chapters, which examine a particular aspect in detail.

Avoiding a Definition

Before examining the history, however, it is worth considering what we mean by 'openness'. It is a term that hides a multitude of interpretations and motives, and this is both its blessing and curse. It is broad enough to be adopted widely, but also loose enough that anyone can claim it, so it becomes meaningless. One solution to this is to adopt a very tight definition. For instance, we might argue that something is only open if it conforms to David Wiley's 4 Rs of Reuse (2007a):

- Reuse – the right to reuse the content in its unaltered/verbatim form (e.g. make a backup copy of the content)
- Revise – the right to adapt, adjust, modify or alter the content itself (e.g. translate the content into another language)
- Remix – the right to combine the original or revised content with other content to create something new (e.g. incorporate the content into a mashup)
- Redistribute – the right to share copies of the original content, your revisions or your remixes with others (e.g. give a copy of the content to a friend)

Wiley added a fifth R, that of 'retain' (the right to make, own and control copies of the content) in 2014 (Wiley 2014). This perspective would posit reuse, and therefore licensing, as the key attribute of openness. The Open Knowledge Foundation proposes a very precise definition of openness, because they are concerned with its misuse. Their definition is: 'A piece of data or content is open if anyone is free to use, reuse and redistribute it – subject only, at most, to the requirement to attribute and/or share-alike.' Each of the key terms is also described in detail (OKF n.d.)

While reuse is undoubtedly significant, it would also ignore some of the broader interpretations of the term, for instance while reuse may be an important aspect of open pedagogy, it also relates to a certain openness in approach, an ethos. A focus purely on reuse gives a content-centric view, and openness relates to practice also. The same is true for any tight definition of 'openness' we might adopt. We lose as much as we gain from restricting ourselves to such a definition. Therefore in this book I will accept that it is a vague term, with a range of definitions, depending on context. As I argue in Chapter 8, my intention is not to set out a rigorous orthodoxy as to what constitutes being open, or to expose open frauds, but to encourage engagement with open practices by academics and institutions.

So, if we reject a single definition of openness, what is the best way to approach it? It is probably a mistake to talk about openness as if it is one unified approach; rather, it is an umbrella term. There may have been a time when it was more unified, particularly in the early stages of the open education movement. To continue the battle metaphor from Chapter 1, early on it was simply a matter of positioning open vs. closed, but as the arguments advance, they become more nuanced. Not only are there different aspects of openness, but it may be that some are mutually exclusive with others, or at least that prioritising some means less emphasis on others. One way of approaching openness is to consider the motivations people have for adopting an open approach. The following are some possibilities for such motivations, but by no means an exclusive list.

- Increased audience – The main aim here is to remove barriers to people accessing a resource, be it an article, book, course, service, video or presentation. This means it has to be free, easily shareable, online, and with easy rights. For example, Davis (2011) found that across 36 journals, those that were published under open access received significantly more downloads and reached a broader audience.

- Increased reuse – This is related to the previous motivation but differs slightly in that here the intention is for others to take what you have created and combine it with other elements, adapt it and republish. The same considerations are required as above, but with an extra emphasis on minimal rights and also creating the resource in convenient chunks that can be adapted. Whereas the first motivation might mean releasing an article online, the second motivation might lead someone to share the data that underlies it.

- Increased access – This is different from the first motivation in that the intention is to reach particular groups who may be disadvantaged. This may mean open access such that no formal entry qualifications are required to study. In this case open is not the same as free, since it may be that such learners require extra support, which is paid for in some way. Helping learners who often fail in formal education has more of a focus on support and less than simply making a resource free. Increased access is not necessarily about price.

- Increased experimentation – One of the reasons many people adopt open approaches is that it allows them to experiment. This can be in the use of different media, creating a different identity or experimenting with an approach that wouldn't fit within the normal constraints of standard practice. For instance, many MOOCs have been using the platform to conduct A/B testing where they tweak one variable across two cohorts, such as the position of a video or the type of feedback given, and investigate its impact (Simonite 2013). The open course creates both the opportunity, with large numbers and frequent presentations, and the ethical framework that permits this. MOOC learners are not paying, so there is a different contract with the institution.

- Increased reputation – Being networked and online can help improve an individual's or an institution's profile. Openness here allows more people to see what they do (the motivation of increased audience) but the main aim is to enhance reputation. As an academic, operating in the open, publishing openly, creating online resources, being active in social media and establishing an online identity can be a good way to achieve peer recognition, which can lead to tangible outputs such as invites to keynotes or research collaborations. Issues of individual reputation and identity are addressed in Chapter 7, on open scholarship.

- Increased revenue – In the previous chapter I raised the issue of openwashing and using openness as a route to commercial success, but it is also true that an open or part-open model can be an effective business model. The freemium approach works this way, where a service is open to a large extent, but some users pay for additional services, with services such as Flickr being an example. If this is the goal, then openness works by creating a significant demand for the product. For universities, this may equate to increased students on formal courses.

- Increased participation – It may be necessary to gather input from an audience without paying to access them. This could be crowdsourcing in research or getting feedback on a book or research proposal. Being open allows others to access it and then provide the input required.

To demonstrate how these different motivations would influence the nature of openness, let us take an imaginary scenario: a university wants to create a MOOC and approaches their educational technologist to come up with a proposal. The university senior management have heard about MOOCs and think they need to be active in this area. They seek the advice of our educational technologist, who consults with a range of different stakeholders and asks them, 'What is the aim of the MOOC? What do you want from it?'

The person from marketing says he wants to increase the university's online profile and reputation. From this perspective the proposed MOOC focuses on a popular subject, featuring a well-known academic. The subject will be 'Life on Mars'. It will be expensive with high-quality production, acting as a showcase for the university and getting it in the press.

When the Dean of the Science faculty is consulted, she says they are concerned about student recruitment on postgraduate courses. They want the MOOC to bring in high-fee paying students from overseas. The model that might work here is one that makes the first six weeks of the existing course open and targets a specific audience, who can then sign up after the first six weeks.

The educational technologist then speaks to an academic who is really keen to try a student-led approach. They feel frustrated by the customer-led focus of conventional teaching and see in MOOCs an opportunity to try some more radical pedagogic approaches that they have been blocked from implementing. They don't see it as particularly massive in terms of audience, but it will be a rich learning experience for those who do it, as the students will be creating the curriculum. This proposal is a MOOC based in Wordpress and featuring a range of technologies with learners co-creating the content.

Later the technologist has a conversation with a funding council who want to bring under-represented groups into science. They will need a lot of support, but they are willing to fund the provision of mentors and support groups in the community. Now they suggest a MOOC based on adapting existing materials, with carefully targeted support and minimal technical barriers.

From each of these perspectives, the resultant MOOC would be very different. It would be open in each of these scenarios, but with a different emphasis on the form that openness should take. Similarly, Haklev (2010) proposes four purposes in the development of OERs, which can be applied to open approaches in general:

- Transformative production – Here the process of production has a transformative effect on those involved. It can be through reflection on the teaching process or exposure to the models of open practice, but the main aim here is to transform an individual or, more usually, an institution's practice.

- Direct use – The aim is for a learner to be able to use the resource independently, so it needs to be complete.
- Reuse – In contrast to the previous purpose, here access by the learner is usually mediated by reuse by another party, such as an educator. Creating material for teachers to use places a different emphasis on the characteristics required than one aimed directly at the end learner.
- Transparency/consultation – The purpose here is to inform users about how the subject is taught.

Motivations may intersect and complement each other. For example, the open textbook movement is largely justified in terms of cost, in that it creates free textbooks and leads to significant savings for students, but there is also the motivation for reuse, since educators are free to adapt the book to their particular needs.

Open Education – A Brief History

When did the current open education movement start? This is a difficult question to answer, as the answer will inevitably be, 'It depends what you mean by the current open education movement.' This response is telling because it illustrates that the open education movement is not easily defined. In fact, like the definition of openness itself, it is probably best viewed not as a single entity but rather a collection of intersecting principles and ideas. This section will draw out these principles and ideas, by focusing on the roots of open education.

I would suggest that there are three key strands that lead to the current set of open education core concepts: open access education, open source software and web 2.0 culture.

Open Universities

Open access to education goes back beyond the foundation of the Open University (OU), with public lectures, but let us take the establishing of the Open University as the start of open access education as it is commonly interpreted. Originally proposed as a 'wireless university' in 1926, the idea gained ground in the early 1960s, and became Labour Party manifesto commitment in 1966 (http://www.open.ac.uk/about/main/the-ou-explained/history-the-ou). It was established in 1969 with the mission statement that it is 'open to people, places, methods and ideas'. The aim of the OU was to open up education to people who were otherwise excluded because they either lacked the qualifications to enter higher education, or their lifestyle and commitments meant they could not commit to full-time education. The university's approach was aimed at removing these barriers. Cormier (2013) suggests the following types of open were important:

> Open = accessible, 'supported open learning', interactive, dialogue. Accessibility was key.

> Open = equal opportunity, unrestricted by barriers or impediments to education and educational resources.

> Open = transparency, sharing educational aims and objectives with students, disclosing marking schemes and offering exam and tutorial advice.

> Open = open entry, most important, no requirement for entrance qualifications. All that was needed were ambition and the will/motivation to learn.

In this interpretation, open education was part-time, distance, supported and open access. The OU model was very successful and a number of other open universities were established in other countries using this as a basis. The need to expand access to higher education to those who could not access the conventional model became something many governments recognised, and the reputation of the OU for high-quality teaching material and good learning experience made the approach respectable. Many of the aims of such open universities, to democratise learning and reach excluded groups, would re-emerge with the arrival of MOOCs (e.g. Koller 2012).

Note that there is no particular stress on free access in this interpretation. Education was to be paid for by the respective government, and open universities were closely allied to whatever form of widening participation they wished to adopt. The emphasis was often on *affordable* education, but before the internet, the other forms of openness were seen as more significant. It was with open source that 'open' and 'free' began to be linked or used synonymously.

Open Source and Free Software

In the 1970s, Richard Stallman, a computer scientist at MIT, became frustrated with the control over computer systems at his institution, and this frustration would lead to a lifelong campaign about the rights associated with software. In 1983 he started the GNU project to develop a rival operating software system to Unix, which would allow users to adapt it as they saw fit. The code for GNU was released openly, in contrast to the standard practice of releasing compiled code, which users cannot access or modify. He saw early on that licenses were the key to the success of the project and championed the copyleft (in contrast with copyright) approach, that allowed users to make changes as long as they acknowledged the original work (Williams 2002). As we shall see, this approach and the GNU licence had a direct link to the open education movement.

Stallman advocated that software should be free in this sense of repurposing and set up the Free Software Foundation in 1985. This is an ideological position about freedom. As the GNU organisation puts it, 'The users (both individually and collectively) control the program and what it does for them. When users don't control the program, the program controls the users.' (http://www.gnu.org/philosophy/free-sw.html). There are four basic freedoms advocated by the free software movement, which echo the 4 Rs of Reuse and later licences in education:

A program is free software if the program's users have the four essential freedoms:

- The freedom to run the program, for any purpose (freedom 0).
- The freedom to study how the program works and change it so it does your computing as you wish (freedom 1). Access to the source code is a precondition for this.
- The freedom to redistribute copies so you can help your neighbour (freedom 2).
- The freedom to distribute copies of your modified versions to others (freedom 3). By doing this you can give the whole community a chance to benefit from your changes. Access to the source code is a precondition for this.

Note that these freedoms are about control, not about cost. Indeed Stallman is quite clear that it does not preclude commercial use and that it is legitimate to purchase 'free' software. The oft quoted phrase is 'freedom as in speech, not as in beer', but this confusion between these two types of 'free' is one that arises repeatedly with regards to open education.

Related to the free software movement was the open source software movement. The two are often combined and referred to as FLOSS (Free/Libre Open Source Software). The open source movement is commonly credited to Eric Raymond, whose essay and book, *The Cathedral and The Bazaar* (2001), set out the principles of the approach. The open source movement, although it has strong principles, can perhaps be best described as a pragmatic approach. Raymond appreciated that software development was nonrivalrous (in that you could give it away and still maintain a copy), and that code could be developed by a community of developers, often working out of their own time and not for financial reward. The driving principle behind open source is that it is more efficient to produce software by making it open. The mantra coined by Raymond is that 'given enough eyeballs, all bugs are shallow'. By making code open then, better software is developed.

The Free Software Foundation make a clear distinction between Free Software and Open Source, stating that:

> [T]he two terms describe almost the same cate-gory of software, but they stand for views based on fundamentally different values. Open source is a develop-ment methodology; free software is a social movement. For the free software movement, free software is an ethi-cal imperative, essential respect for the users' freedom. By contrast, the philosophy of open source considers issues in terms of how to make software 'better' (Stall-man 2012).

Raymond himself emphasises the practical nature of open source, stating that 'To me, Open Source is not particularly a moral or a legal issue. It's an engineering issue. I advocate Open Source, because very pragmatically, I think it leads to better engineering results and better economic results' (Raymond 2002).

To non-developers this distinction often seems pedantic or obtuse. The two are generally clumped together, and indeed many open source advocates are passionate about freedoms also. It is worth noting the difference, however, as it has resonance with the motivations in open education. Openness in education can be seen as a practical approach; for instance, the learning object movement of the early 2000s often used the argument of efficiency, as we shall see in the next chapter. But the 'social' argument is also at the core of open education, making the outputs of publicly funded research available to all, rather than in proprietary databases.

The free and open source software movements can be seen as creating the context within which open education could flourish, partly by analogy, and partly by establishing a precedent. But there is also a very direct link. David Wiley (2008) reports how in 1998 he became interested in developing an open licence for educational content and contacted both Stallman and Raymond directly. Out of this came the open content licence, which he developed with publishers to establish the Open Publication Licence (OPL). This licence had two forms: form A, which prohibited the distribution of modified versions without the permission of the author; and form B, which prohibited the distribution of the book in paper form for commercial purposes. As Wiley comments, this naming convention wasn't useful, as it didn't tell you what the licence referred to, and similarly, the badges didn't tell you which of the two had been selected. But it was adopted by O'Reilly press, and became the forerunner to a more widely adopted licence.

The OPL proved to be one of the key components, along with the Free Software Foundation's GNU licence, in the development of the Creative Commons licences by Larry Lessig and others in 2002 (Geere 2011). These addressed some of the issues of the open content licence and went on to become essential in the open education. The simple licences in Creative Commons (CC) allow users to easily share resources and isn't restricted to software code. The user can determine the conditions under which it can be used – the default is that it always acknowledges the creator (CC-BY), but further restrictions exist, such as preventing commercial use without the creator's permission (CC-NC). The Creative Commons licences are permissive rather than restrictive. They allow the user to do what the licence permits without seeking permission. They don't forbid other uses, such as commercial use for a CC-NC licence; they simply say you need to contact the creator first. These licences have been a very practical requirement for the OER movement to persuade institutions and individuals to release content openly, with the knowledge that their intellectual property is still maintained.

The direct connection to Tim O'Reilly segues into the next influential development, as it was O'Reilly who coined the term 'web 2.0'.

Web 2.0

Although it is a phrase that has now been through the peak of popularity and passed into history, the web 2.0 phenomenon of the mid '00s had a significant impact on the nature of openness in education. The term was used to recognise a growing development in the way in which people were using the web. It wasn't a deliberate movement, but rather a means of distinguishing the more read/write, user-generated nature of a number of tools and approaches.

In 2005 Tim O'Reilly outlined eight principles of web 2.0, which characterised the way tools were developing and being used. This included sites such as Wikipedia, Flickr and YouTube. Some of the principles turned out to be more significant than others, and some related more to developers than users, but they encapsulated a way of using the internet that shifted from a broadcast to a conversational model. This set of developments would later combine with social media such as Twitter and Facebook.

In terms of open education, the web 2.0 movement was significant for two major reasons. Firstly, it decentralised much of the engagement with the web. Educators didn't need to get approval to create websites; they could set up a blog, establish a Twitter account, create YouTube videos and share their presentations on Slideshare independently. This created a culture of openness amongst those academics who adopted such approaches, and this would often lead to engagement with open education in some form. We shall look at this in more detail in chapter 7 when online identity is considered. Secondly, it created a context where open and free were seen as the default characteristics of online material. Users, be they educators, students, potential students or the general public, had an expectation that content they encountered online was freely accessible.

Coalescing Principles

From these three main strands – open universities, open source and web 2.0 – a number of principles coalesce into the current open education movement. From open universities we have the principles of open access and removal of barriers to education. This was restricted to a particular interpretation of open education, however, and closely allied with particular national policies. Open source software gives us principles of freedom of use, mutual benefit in sharing resources and the significance of licences. This didn't spread much beyond the specialised community of software developers. Lastly, web 2.0 provides the cultural context within which the openness becomes widely recognised and expected. A list of general principles inherited from these three strands might be:

- Freedom to reuse
- Open access
- Free cost
- Easy use
- Digital, networked content
- Social, community based approaches
- Ethical arguments for openness
- Openness as an efficient model

These are digital, networked transformations; the nonrivalrous nature of digital content and the easy distribution of content and conversations online, underlies all of them. And while it is possible to think of them as a cluster of interconnecting principles, there are camps, or smaller clusters, within this general grouping. For instance, the notion that content should be free in terms of price was not a driving concern of the open universities or the open source software movement, although open source software often is free. It was with the development of web 2.0 that free became an expectation. One can see the various aspects of openness in education as aligning themselves with some of these principles, but not all of them. For instance, the commercial MOOCs are taking the free cost and open access element, but not necessarily the freedom to reuse. It is because of this blend of principles that I have resisted a simple definition of openness in education and would rather propose it is best viewed as this collection of overlapping principles.

Conclusions

Openness in education has many strands leading to it, and depending on the particular flavour of open education one is considering, some of these will be more prevalent than others. This makes talking about open education as a clearly defined entity or movement problematic, and adopting a single definition is counterproductive. Just as open education has many inter-related aspects, such as open access, OER, MOOCs and open scholarship, so it is defined by overlapping but distinct influences. In this chapter three such influences, namely open universities, open source and web 2.0 have been proposed, but there will be others, for example, from a socio-political perspective. Some have detected elements of neo-liberalism in the popularity of MOOCs (Hall 2013). It is not the intention of this book to explore these aspects, although such an analysis with regards to open education would be fruitful.

Having looked at the possible motivations for the open approach, and the influencing factors that have led to its current configuration, the different aspects of openness in education can now be considered. The first of these is perhaps the most venerable, that of open access publishing, which is the subject of the next chapter.

CHAPTER 3

Open Access Publishing

One must be prepared to fight for one's simple pleasures and to defend them against elegance and erudition and all manner of glamorous enticements.

—Amor Towles

Introduction

In Chapter 1 the argument was put forward that we have witnessed the transition of openness from peripheral interest to mainstream approach in higher education. This transition brings with it a new set of tensions and issues, as was seen in the analogy of political revolutions and the green movement. Having explored the concept of openness in more detail in the previous chapter, the next 5 chapters represent the core of the argument set out in Chapter 1. Each chapter will take an aspect of open education and detail how it has been successful and the key challenges it now faces. This commences in this chapter with a very successful aspect of open education, namely open access publishing.

In the battle for open, open access (OA) publishing is probably the area with the longest history. It's worth looking at the issues that are arising here before considering other aspects of open education, as it exhibits the characteristics of the battle for openness that were set out in Chapter 1. For example, there is considerable money involved in the industry. Reed Elsevier reported revenue of over £6 billion in 2012, of which over £2 billion was for Science, Technical and Medical publishing. It's an area where openness has 'won', to a large extent, with mandates from research funders, government and institutions which make open access publishing compulsory. And yet at the time of victory, open access advocates are also beset with doubt and conflict.

The Gold route is to make journals open access, so any reader can access the content free of charge. The focus of the Gold route is on using journals as the means to share content. There are different ways that such journals can be funded; for example, a university or professional society might fund the journal itself. If it is a journal published by an existing publisher, then the usual route is that of Article Process Charges (APCs), where the author (or the research funder) pays a charge for making the article open. The Gold route is favoured by many mandates, but with APCs, it may well end up costing more both financially and in terms of opportunity, as will be explored below.

An open access 'sting' operation published in *Science* (Bohannon 2013), where an obviously flawed, fake article was accepted by 157 OA journals, demonstrated that this pay-to-publish model may create a tension in the relationship with the publisher. This sting was revealing with regards to the battle for open for two reasons. Firstly, it demonstrated again that 'openness' has market value as a term, and so dubious journals have entered the marketplace offering open access publishing. Secondly, the incumbents (many of whom published the article) may not have a vested interest in making OA a success. If OA is perceived as lower quality, then it reinforces their market position and the position of the existing library subscription model. This illustrates the danger of trying to let commercial interests shape the direction of openness. Before we consider this, however, let us look first at how open access publishing has been so successful.

The Success of Open Access

Open Access publishing began in the 1990s, as we have seen, taking its inspiration from open source communities, and also by realising that digital, networked content changed the nature of publication. Open Access is usually interpreted to mean 'free online access to scholarly works', although the Budapest Open Access Initiative (2002) gives a more formal definition, which encompasses not only free access in terms of cost, but free from copyright constraints also:

> By 'open access' to this literature, we mean its free availability on the public internet, permitting any users to read, download, copy, distribute, print, search, or link to the full texts of these articles, crawl them for indexing, pass them as data to software, or use them for any other lawful purpose, without financial, legal, or technical barriers other than those inseparable from gaining access to the internet itself. The only constraint on reproduction and distribution, and the only role for copyright in this domain, should be to give authors control over the integrity of their work and the right to be properly acknowledged and cited.

This echoes the distinction between free cost and free reuse that Stallman sought to make with regards to software. While the definition of open access is not as contentious as other terms we will encounter, the route to it is. There are two main methods by which open access is realised:

- The Gold route, where the publishers make a journal (or an article) open access. For commercial publishers, fees received through the proprietary model from library subscriptions must be recouped, so an APC is levied. A study of 1,370 journals published in 2010 found the range to be between US$8 and US$3,900 with an average APC of US$906 (Solomon & Bjork 2012). The Gold route need not require APCs, however. That is just one model of making it viable.
- The Green route, where the author self archives a copy of the article, either on their own site or on an institutional repository.

With Gold, the emphasis is on the journal, and with Green, on repositories. To these a third option is sometimes added, termed the 'Platinum route', whereby the journal does not make any APC and publishes open access, but this could be seen as a variant on the Gold route. Such journals are usually operated by societies or universities, where financial return is a lower priority than dissemination.

But there is further complexity to this picture also. With regards to the Green route, what constitutes 'green' can vary. Many publishers will place an embargo for a set period, meaning that an article cannot be self-archived until this has passed, which can range from six to eighteen months. In its open access mandate, the US Office of Science and Technology Policy (OSTP) allows a 12 month embargo (Holdren 2013), while Science Europe (2013) advocates only 6 months. The Gold route can be used in hybrid mode, whereby certain articles in a journal are open access, but not all of them. In this model, publishers still charge the subscription fee for the journal overall, although this may be lowered, as well as receiving APCs for individual articles. This is seen as a model for transition to open access, but others argue it is simply a means of gaining revenue twice for the same journal (Harnard 2012). Science Europe takes an unequivocal stand against the hybrid model, stating that the hybrid model 'as currently defined and implemented by publishers, is not a working and viable pathway to Open Access. Any model for transition to Open Access supported by Science Europe Member Organisations must prevent "double dipping" and increase cost transparency.' Regarding rights, it is still possible for an article to be openly available, but the definitions of open access stress that reuse is required, so the use of Creative Commons licences is the norm.

The uptake of open access has been very successful. Laakso et al. (2011) plot the growth of OA journals and articles since the 1990s, as shown in **Figure 1**.

Similarly, the University of Southampton's ROARMAP project (Registry of Open Access Repositories Mandatory Archiving Policies) plots the number of open access policies at institutional, funder and thesis level. The pattern here is delayed somewhat from that seen with OA journals, as policies only came into place once OA was an established practice, but they show the same pattern of substantial growth from 2003 to 2013 (**Figure 2**).

The trends from both appear to be in one direction, and there is no immediate reason to suppose they will plateau or decline. A recent report from Wiley found that 59% of authors had published in OA journals, the first time the proportion has exceeded half (Warne 2013). Open access publishing is not a minority pursuit any more, reserved for those with a particular zeal for it; it has moved into mainstream practice. This follows the pattern set out in Chapter 1.

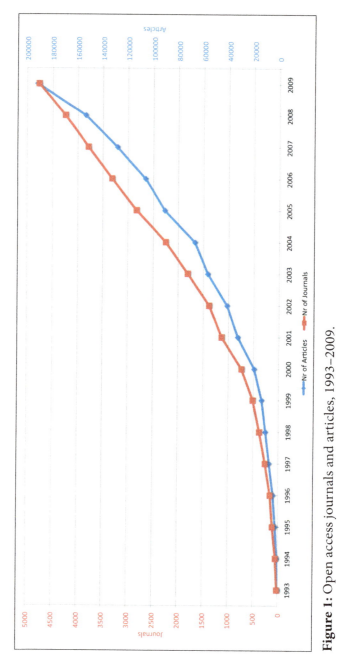

Figure 1: Open access journals and articles, 1993–2009. *Source:* Laakso et al. 2011. Published under a CC-BY license.

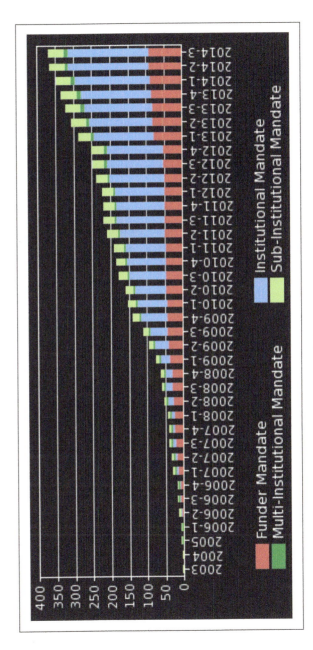

Figure 2: Uptake of open access policies, 2003–2013.
Source: ROARMAP. Published under a CC-BY license.

Before examining the issues that OA now faces, it is worth considering why it has seen such positive uptake. The arguments for open access fall broadly into two camps, which reflect those of the free and open source movements – it is an effective mode of operation, and it has a strong ethical basis.

It can be seen as effective from the perspective of the author who wants their work to be as widely read and cited as possible. It would seem logical that articles which are published without any access restrictions would receive greater attention than those published in proprietary databases, which need to be accessed through libraries (or purchased on an article by article basis). From the web 2.0 influence on open education, we know there is an expectation that content will be free, and so any reader encountering an article that requires payment will simply look elsewhere. Social media can also be seen to impose an open access pressure on articles. In order for resources to be shared effectively via Twitter or other means, the article has to be openly available. It is of little use sharing a link to an interesting article if it then requires others to pay US$50 to access it.

Even if the majority of readers are academics, their host institutions may not always have access to that particular journal. Since 2001 (Lawrence 2001) there has been a growing body of evidence that openly available articles have higher downloads and citations than those in proprietary databases, as Gargouri et al. (2010) summarise: 'This "OA Impact Advantage" has been found in all fields analyzed so far – physical, technological, biological and social sciences, and humanities'. The Open Citation Project (2013) has a comprehensive bibliography of studies that demonstrate this effect. Some studies report that citations are not increased, but the number of downloads are, often by substantial percentages, for instance Davis et al. (2008) found 89% more full-text downloads for open access articles.

In examining the motivations academics have for publishing in peer reviewed journals, Hemmings et al. (2006) suggest three categories of factors: incentive, pressure and support. Incentive was the most salient of these and could take intrinsic forms, such as sharing findings, and extrinsic forms, such as increased chances of promotion. Given that academics are very rarely paid for contributions, then the open access impact advantage benefits this motivation of incentive – whether the main appeal is to increase interest in the area or to improve an individual's profile, then increasing the number of downloads and citations of an article will likely benefit these aims. This is only countered by the prestige of publishing in certain journals, whether they are open or not.

Open access publishing operates as an efficient, pragmatic model for disseminating research findings, which is the primary function of academic publishing. It also has a strong ethical, or ideological, argument, since much of the funding for the research that is published in journals comes from public sources. This forms a central tenet of most open access mandates; for example, the Wellcome Trust (n.d.), a charity which funds medical research, states that it 'believes that maximising the distribution of these papers – by providing free, online access – is the most effective way of ensuring that the research we fund can be accessed, read and built upon.'

The US OSTP policy (Holdren, *2013*) states that 'the direct results of federally funded scientific research are made available to and useful for the public, industry, and the scientific community'. There is a straightforward argument here that if the public are paying for research, then they should have access to it. There is also a more general argument that research progresses by making it available to as many as people as possible, and that access to any research (regardless of who the funder is) should be made as available as possible. Mike Taylor (2013a) puts it bluntly: 'Publishing science behind paywalls is immoral.'

The combination of these practical and ethical arguments has made the existing practices and profits of academic publishers increasingly difficult to justify and maintain. As we shall see with other aspects of openness, the argument becomes irresistible. This is when the real battle for open begins, as we shall now see.

The Finch Report

The Finch report was the result of a working group set up by the UK government to make recommendations regarding open access publishing, led by Dame Janet Finch. The group published their report in July 2012, recommending a transition to an open access environment and backing the Gold route to publish (Finch Group 2012). The report's recommendations were accepted by the Government, although a later Short Inquiry was held to examine some of the implementation details. A fund of £10M was made available to help universities transition to Gold route open access.

Although it is UK-focused, the Finch report represents a microcosm of some of the issues in open education, and so is worth considering in detail, as it is a pattern seen elsewhere. At first glance it looks like a remarkable success for the open access advocates. Not only has the recommendation come down strongly in favour of open access, but the Government has accepted this and even made funds available to support it. But a closer analysis of the report and implementation raises a number of concerns.

The first concern is the caution inherent in the project. The report acknowledges that some repositories such as arXiv (the physics pre-publication repository) have been successful but concludes they are not a viable model on their own, stating that there is a:

> widespread acknowledgement that repositories on their own do not provide a sustainable basis for a research communications system that seeks to provide access to quality-assured content; for they do not themselves provide any arrangements for pre-publication peer review.

> Rather, they rely on a supply of published material that has been subject to peer review by others; or in some cases they provide facilities for comments and ratings by readers that may constitute a more informal system of peer review once the material has been deposited and disseminated via the repository itself.

However, this is a statement of the current position. If a national initiative is being proposed, then a repository (or collection of repositories) may well be a viable approach. The recommendation to move to Gold open access means that effectively the taxpayer will be funding publishers, since the money will come from research bodies. Viewing this money as possible expenditure to be allocated to open access then it could be usefully spent on a national, interdisciplinary arXiv. Green OA advocate Harnad (2012) argues that Green OA is free, and that the Finch report's Gold OA will cost £50–60M annually to implement, and criticises Finch for not backing this model.

The second concern is the lack of demand the report places on publishers. The report suggests that it would be good for publishers to link data with publications, but does not mandate it:

> In an ideal world, there would be closer integration between the text and the data presented in journal articles, with seamless links to interactive datasets; a

> consequent fall in the amount of supplementary material; and two-way links, with interactive viewers, between publications and relevant data held in data archives. The availability of, and access to, publications and associated data would then become fully integrated and seamless, with both feeding off each other.

The report could recommend funding universities to directly publish OA journals (as set out below), where an author would get the 'basic' package, and commercial publishers can add value to this. Without mandating what is required for the Gold route or what is a reasonable fee to charge, it creates a financial situation that may be worse for universities and funders than the current model.

The Finch report has one further problem, which is the strong influence of publishers in establishing the recommendations. Maintaining the economic viability of the academic publishing industry as it stands is a key objective. For example, the report states:

> arrangements must be in place to enable publishers (whether they are in the commercial or the not-for-profit sector) to meet the legitimate costs of peer review, production, and marketing, as well as high standards of presentation, discoverability and navigation, together with the kinds of linking and enrichment of texts ('semantic publishing') that researchers and other readers increasingly expect. Publishers also need to generate surpluses for investment in innovation and new services; for distribution as profits to shareholders …

Generating profits for publishers and shareholders should be seen as a side effect of providing a useful service, but it should not be a *goal*. The goal is to effectively disseminate research.

The danger of this influence is that it creates an economically unviable model, where much of the money flows to shareholders, or creating systems that gain competitive advantage. Neither of these are concerns for disseminating research. A Deutsche bank report (cited inMcGuigan and Russell 2008) stated that:

> We believe the publisher adds relatively little value to the publishing process. We are not attempting to dismiss what 7,000 people at the publishers do for a living. We are simply observing that if the process really were as complex, costly and value-added as the publishers protest that it is, 40% margins wouldn't be available.

The conclusion of the Finch report (and the subsequent update does not substantially change it) does nothing to address this, and indeed could make the situation worse. It also loses an opportunity to think of more radical methods through which that principle aim of disseminating research might be achieved, because the stability of the existing approach is assumed.

The Gold Route

One of the criticisms of Finch is its support for the Gold route to open access publishing. As mentioned, advocates of the Green route argue that this is both surer and cheaper. However, the Gold route is not inherently flawed; it is more a matter of which economic model is adopted and the price and freedom the model offers. As such, the debate around the Gold route provides an example of the finer details around openness that only come into focus once the initial open approach has been accepted. One reason for this disquiet around Gold OA is that it is a method being determined by the publishing industry and not by academics themselves. This may have a number of unintended consequences.

Ironically, openness may lead to elitism. If an author needs to pay to publish, then, particularly in times of austerity, it becomes something of a luxury. New researchers or smaller universities won't have these funds available. Many publishers have put in waivers for new researchers; PLoS for example, has a 'no questions asked' waiver and has no fee for developing countries. There is, however, no guarantee of these, and if Gold OA funded by APCs becomes the norm, then it may be in conflict with commercial publishers' need to maximise profits. If there are sufficient paying customers, then it's not in their interest to grant too many waivers. It also means richer universities can flood journals with articles. Similarly, those with research grants can publish, as this is where the funding will come from, and those without may find themselves excluded. This will increase competition in an already highly competitive research funding regime. Open access could increase the 'Matthew Effect', whereby the same authors publish more articles (Anderson 2012). It would indeed be a strange irony if open access ended up creating a self-perpetuating elite.

Another potential issue with Gold OA funded through APCs is that it may create additional cost. Once the cost of publishing is shifted to research funders, then the author doesn't have a vested interest in the price. There is no strong incentive to keep costs down or find alternative funding mechanisms. The cost for publication is shifted to taxpayers (who ultimately fund research) or students (if it comes out of university money). The profits and benefits stay with the publishers who continue as before but with perhaps even less restraint.

The final reservation I have regarding Gold OA as it is commonly interpreted is that it doesn't promote change. In *The*

Digital Scholar (2011), I discussed how a digital, networked and open approach could alter our interpretation of what constitutes research and that much of our current perception was dictated by existing output forms. So, for instance, we could see smaller granularity of outputs than the traditional 5,000 word article; greater use of post-review instead of pre-review; and adoption of different media formats, all of which begin to change our concept of what constitutes research. But a Gold OA model that reinforces the power of commercial publishers simply maintains a status quo and keeps the peer-reviewed article as the primary focus of research that must be attained.

It is still too early to know if any of these scenarios will come to pass, but they are entirely feasible, and if they did arise then it would be difficult to portray open access as having realised any form of victory. However, it does not necessarily follow that Harnad's view that Green OA is the only route is correct. Rather we should view the current debate around Gold OA as being symptomatic of changing relationships with publishers.

The Publisher Relationship

In 2008, Cambridge University Press, Oxford University Press and Sage took a court action against Georgia State University for using their content unlicensed in 'e-reserves' for its students, claiming this went beyond fair use. In 2012 over 14,000 academics joined a boycott of publisher Elsevier, protesting about their 'exorbitantly high' charges and practices, which they saw as limiting the free exchange of knowledge (Cost of Knowledge 2012). In 2013 Elsevier sent 'take-down notices' to the academic social media site Academia.edu, demanding that copies of articles that were shared on academic profiles on the site be removed (Taylor 2013b).

However you view these events individually, they seem symptomatic of an increasingly dysfunctional relationship between academics and publishers. This wasn't always the case; what had been a mutually beneficial relationship has begun to feel more exploitative. As Edwards and Shulenberger(2002) put it: 'Beginning in the late 1960s and early '70s, this gift exchange began to break down. A few commercial publishers recognized that research generated at public expense and given freely for publication by the authors represented a commercially exploitable commodity.'

Why did this happen? Part of the reason was the shift to digital. In the last chapter I stressed that the digital, networked nature of open education was fundamental. The open access publishing field demonstrates why it is so important. In theory, the same restrictions existed previously under the print model, but when academics had no real control over the distribution channel, it didn't matter in any practical sense. Signing copyright forms with publishers meant surrendering film or merchandise rights, but Hollywood rarely came calling for academic authors, so it had no practical impact. Authors were free to distribute photocopies on request or to use them in their own teaching. Given the barriers to distributing copies, this had no impact on the publishers, so author and publisher could exist in a reasonably mutually beneficial relationship. But once the content became digital and could be freely distributed, the nature of this relationship changed and the interests of each party became antagonistic. The author now wants to retain the right to freely distribute as before, but now that the barriers to doing so have been removed, the damage to the business of the publisher is more substantial.

In each of the examples of conflict I stated at the beginning of this section, it is the digital, networked nature of the publishing approach that is at the heart of the dispute. The takedown notices issued to Academia.edu by Elsevier offer a revealing example of how this has changed the relationship. Creating a profile on Academia.edu can be seen as one route to establishing an online identity for an academic (we will look at identity in more detail later). An academic's publications form a key part of that professional identity. In a digital, networked context it makes sense for the individual academic to use this site to construct a central hub for their online identity, including access to all their publications. From Elsevier's perspective, this means Academia.edu is acting as an unlicensed distributor of their content, potentially damaging their revenue. If we see the establishment of an online identity as now an essential part of what it means to be an academic (as I argue in Chapter 7), then these two demands are now in conflict in a way they weren't previously.

In addition to conflicts with existing publishers, open access has led to new entrants who are deemed 'predatory'. These journals often seek contributions and then charge high APCs, and have low academic standards. Beall (2010) characterises them as follows: 'They work by spamming scholarly e-mail lists, with calls for papers and invitations to serve on nominal editorial boards... Also, these publishers typically provide little or no peer review. In fact, in most cases, their peer review process is a facade' On his website, Scholarly Open Access (http://scholarlyoa.com), Beall provides a list of predatory journals and also criteria for determining these. Another practice that has arisen is that of 'journal hijacking', where an old, existing journal is used to create a false online version to lure potential contributors, again using the Gold OA method to extract money.

So with existing publishers on one side demanding high fees for open access, whilst also continuing with subscription models, and predatory journals seeking to swindle money from authors on the other, it can feel to many authors that open access has not improved the practice of publishing at all. This is a reminder of the lessons we saw from other victories in Chapter 1 – victory doesn't feel like victory should. However, it isn't always this way, and there are examples of good practice, as well as a range of opportunities, which will be explored next.

New Models of Publishing

A number of publishers have sought to redefine (or reset) the relationship with academic authors to a more cooperative one. The traditional model of physical printing meant that part of the contract was about the creation of a product. In a digital environment where templates can be used to easily create an online journal, the focus shifts away from the product and more to the services the publisher offers.

Publishers such as PLoS and Ubiquity offer Gold OA, but at relatively low cost, and with waivers for those who cannot afford to pay. Such publishers often use open source software (reinforcing the influence of that domain in open education), such as Open Journal Systems (OJS) or Ambra. The use of such software over bespoke, proprietary systems developed by commercial publishers offers considerable financial benefits (Clarke 2007) and also gives access to a community of developers.

The fee paid to such publishers is essentially to cover a set of services, including copyediting, administration and dissemination (for example registering journals with databases). This allows universities to make a clear decision as to whether the cost of these services is reasonable compared with publishing themselves. This brings us onto a second model: that of the university press.

University presses were established to distribute books and journals where the commercial interest was not deemed strong enough. Oxford University first published in 1478 and the US Cambridge Press in 1640. Givler (2002) says the motivation for founding modern university presses was that 'to leave the publication of scholarly, highly specialized research to the workings of a commercial marketplace would be, in effect, to condemn it to languish unseen.' There was a regular growth in presses, with one a year opening from 1920 to 1970 (Givler, *2002*). The university press survived well to the beginning of the 21st century, when increased competition from commercial publishers impacted their viability. This competition was driven partly by significant hedge fund investment making it difficult for university presses, with limited funds, to compete. They were caught in a pincer movement of decreasing financial support from universities dealing with the financial crisis and increased competition from commercial publishers for their business (Greco and Wharton 2010).

One of the problems with the finances was that printing and distributing paper journals was an alien business for universities to be in. It involved equipment and logistics which were costly to maintain and seemed increasingly detached from the everyday business of the university. But the almost wholesale shift to online journals and print-on-demand (POD) books has now seen a realignment with university skills and functions. Universities do run websites, and they are the places people look to for information. The experience the higher education sector has built up through OERs (the subject of the next chapter), software development and website maintenance now aligns beneficially with the skills they've always had of editing, reviewing, writing and managing journals. So now could be the time for the rebirth of the university press as a place that runs a set of open access online journals.

Running journals on an *ad hoc* basis across universities is inefficient. By centralising resources in website maintenance and administration, a university could support several journals. The other main roles are those that are currently performed by academics for free anyway – reviewing, managing and editing the journal, organising special editions, etc.

The same universities are currently paying a considerable sum to publishers through libraries. By withdrawing some of this expense and reallocating it to internal publishing, then the university could cover these costs. In addition, the university gains kudos and recognition for its journals and the expertise and control is maintained within the university. If enough universities do this, each publishing four or more journals, then the university presses can begin to cover the range of expertise required.

This is, of course, happening at many universities, but it's a piecemeal approach, often operating in the spare time of people with other jobs. One has only to look at thelist of journals currently using OJSto see that it's an approach that is growing. Universities may outsource the 'back-office' functions to a publisher like Ubiquity, while still maintaining control of the editorial function of the journals.

Frances Pinter of Knowledge Unlatched (n.d.) is seeking to create a library consortium to pay for the creation of open access publications (http://www.knowledgeunlatched.org/about/how-it-works/). This model takes a global view and reflects that libraries are currently purchasing material produced by academics from third-party publishers, so a redefinition of this approach would be for the libraries to allocate those funds directly to the publication of the content under an open access licence (which they or others then do not need to purchase).

In the US in particular there has also been a movement to create Open Textbooks, through initiatives such as OpenStax. These aim to create open access textbooks for core subjects such as statistics, and thus remove the considerable cost of buying text books for undergraduate students. Open textbooks overlap with OERs, so we will look at them in more detail in the next chapter.

This is not to suggest that any of these approaches is the 'correct' path to pursue but rather to illustrate possible models of open access publishing. What all these approaches have in common is that openness is central to their approach, it is not an attempt to (often begrudgingly) graft open access onto existing practices, with the aim of disturbing these as little as possible.

Conclusions

The intention of this chapter was not to provide a comprehensive account of open access publishing models, licences and economics, but rather to illustrate how open access demonstrates many of the key characteristics of the battle for open. The first of these characteristics is the considerable victory of the open access approach with it being mandated in several countries, and increasingly popular amongst academics. The second is that these changes are driven by the general principles of openness we saw in the previous chapter, such as the freedom to reuse digital, networked content, ethical arguments for openness and openness as an efficient model.

The third characteristic is the downside of this victory, with new areas of tension and conflict, as represented by debates around the Gold OA route, embargoes for self-archiving, and predatory entrants into the market. Lastly, the importance of engagement and ownership of the process by academics is highlighted by the potential models that open practices offer.

In his book *What Money Can't Buy*, Sandel (2012) explores the increasing market-based approach to much of society. His examples include paying homeless people to queue in line for others and a nursery that when it started charging fees for late collection of children, found that the late collections increased. Behaviours that had been ruled by social conventions became monetised and could be purchased. Sandel might well have added the changing nature of the relationship with academic publishers to his list. Once authors start paying publishers directly to publish, as is the case with Gold route, then as Sandel argues, this fundamentally changes the nature of the relationship. Academic publishing is a practice that is at the core of academic identity, and as such, this fundamental change in its nature illustrates the impact of openness, and the importance of engaging with its future direction.

If open access publishing is the most established area for open education, then open educational resources runs a close second and offers a comparative study of a movement being owned largely by universities themselves. This will be the focus of the next chapter.

CHAPTER 4

Open Educational Resources

To understand the world at all, sometimes you could only focus on a tiny bit of it.

—Donna Tartt

Introduction

Having looked at open access publishing in the previous chapter, an area where the tensions around the directions of openness are evident, this chapter continues to flesh out the central proposal that openness has been successful but now faces a battle over its future direction. In this chapter we will examine an area that provides a useful contrast to open access, namely that of open educational resources (OERs). Whereas open access sees educators attempting to wrestle control back from third-party publishers and often places the two in conflict with each other, the OER movement has largely developed from within the higher education sector. There are commercial offerings in this space, many allied to the publishers we encountered in the previous chapter, but ownership of the OER movement resides within the education sector still. One area where the type of tension seen in the previous chapter is encountered is in open access textbooks, which are addressed in a separate section below. Here OERs overlap with open access publishing. At the other end of the spectrum, there is sequencing of OERs to create a course, where there is overlap with the subject of the next chapter, MOOCs. This raises the issue of definition – what do we mean by an OER – and to answer that, we will first look at a brief history of the OER movement.

Learning Objects

The OER movement grew out of earlier work around 'learning objects', and many of the benefits of OER were claimed for learning objects, so it is worth examining them first. As elearning moved into the mainstream (around the year 2000), educators and institutions found they were creating often expensive learning resources from scratch. In Chapter 2 some of the influences from other fields were examined, and one such lesson from the open source movement was the efficiency in reusing parts of software code. If you want a map, a spell-checker or a style sheet, then it makes sense to take an existing one and simply call to it from your program, rather than developing one from scratch. This same relentless logic suggested that, with the digitisation of content, useful resources could be shared between institutions. This led to interest in what were termed 'learning objects' (or to stress their recyclable value, 'reusable learning objects').

Stephen Downes (2001) set out the compelling economic argument for learning objects:

> [T]here are thousands of colleges and universities, each of which teaches, for example, a course in introductory trigonometry. Each such trigonometry course in each of these institutions describes, for example, the sine wave

function. Moreover, because the properties of sine wave functions remains constant from institution to institution, we can assume that each institution's description of sine wave functions is more or less the same as other institutions'. What we have, then, are thousands of similar descriptions of sine wave functions…

Now for the premise: the world does not need thousands of similar descriptions of sine wave functions available online. Rather, what the world needs is one, or maybe a dozen at most, descriptions of sine wave functions available online. …

Suppose that just one description of the sine wave function is produced. A high-quality and fully interactive piece of learning material could be produced for, perhaps, $1,000. If 1,000 institutions share this one item, the cost is $1 per institution. But if each of a thousand institutions produces a similar item, then each institution must pay $1,000, with a resulting total expenditure of $1,000,000. For one lesson. In one course.

It sounds irresistible doesn't it? And yet, despite investment and research, the vision of a large pool of shareable learning objects never materialised. It is briefly worth considering why this was the case, as the reasons will be relevant for later manifestations of open education.

The first reason that learning objects failed to achieve their desired critical mass was what Wiley (2004) termed 'the reusability paradox'. Wiley contends that context is what makes learning meaningful for people, so the more context a learning object has, the more useful it is for a learner. If we take Downes's sine wave example, it is not just the sine wave function that is useful, but placing it in context, for example, making linkage with previous content. Arguably, content with clear boundaries, such as a sine wave function, can be easily separated and then re-embedded in other courses, where these connections are made, but this becomes more difficult for subjects with less well-defined boundaries, for example taking a learning object about slavery from one context and embedding it elsewhere may lose much of the context required for it to be meaningful. While learners want context, in order for them to be reusable, learning objects should have as little context as possible, as this reduces the opportunities for their reuse. This leads to Wiley's paradox, which he summarises as, 'It turns out that reusability and pedagogical effectiveness are completely orthogonal to each other. Therefore, pedagogical effectiveness and potential for reuse are completely at odds with one another.' This is shown in **Figure 3**.

A second issue with learning objects was over-specification. At the time of their development, interoperability was a major concern, so being able to take a learning object developed by one university, and use it in the learning management system (LMS) of another one was the goal. There were issues around discoverability also, as much

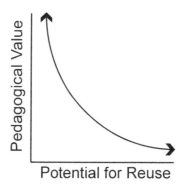

Figure 3: The Reusability Paradox.
Figure by Wiley 2004. Published under a CC-BY license.

of this predated the dominance of Google. This led to the development of a range of standards, all with the noble intention of making learning objects more discoverable and reusable. The problem with this approach was that the standards became so complex that they became a barrier to adoption for most academics.

A third significant factor was the sustainability of the approach. Although it made economic and pedagogic sense to develop high-quality learning objects, they required a critical mass in order to be useful for educators. And achieving this proved problematic. The barriers created by the standards were off-putting for many educators. More significantly, sharing teaching outputs by contributing to learning object repositories was not part of standard educational practice in the way that sharing research findings through articles was. Acquiring a wide range of objects that would meet the needs of educators became difficult to realise.

These three factors, reusability, standardisation and culture, would partly be addressed by developments both inside and outside education. Some, however, were largely forgotten and are now being 'rediscovered', particularly with regards to MOOCs, as we shall see in the next chapter. So while learning objects faltered, in some respects they can be viewed as the required first steps in the process of opening up educational content, and were simply too early. The problem of over-complex standards for instance was largely overcome with the web 2.0 developments of simple embedding and tagging. Contributing a set of teaching materials to a learning object repository and being required to make it compliant with a standard such as SCORM (Sharable Content Object Reference Model) and adding a set of metadata may make it very reusable, but the complexity outweighed the benefit. Compare this with saving a PowerPoint file to the Slideshare site and tagging it with a few keywords, which was an activity educators took to readily.

OERs

In 2001 the OER movement began in earnest when MIT announced its OpenCourseWare initiative. MIT's goal was to make all the learning materials used by their 1800 courses available via the internet, where the resources could be used and repurposed as desired by others, without charge. The William and Flora Hewlett Foundation, who funded the MIT project, define OERs as:

> teaching, learning, and research resources that reside in the public domain or have been released under an intellectual property license that permits their free use and re-purposing by others. Open educational resources include full courses, course materials, modules, textbooks, streaming videos, tests, software, and any other tools, materials, or techniques used to support access to knowledge (Hewlett Foundation n.d.).

This is a broad definition that covers whole courses (MOOCs) as well as individual resources, textbooks and software. A key element to it is the stress on the license that permits free use and re-purposing. This again draws on the open source distinction between free as in beer and free as in speech. In order to satisfy the Hewlett definition it is not enough to simply be free (as many MOOCs are), it has to be reusable also. There are other definitions of OERs available (see Creative Commons 2013a for a comparison of these) but even if they do not explicitly mandate an open license, they all emphasise the right to reuse content.

The OpenCourseWare initiative also addressed some of the issues seen with learning objects, particularly that of sustainability, since it took existing teaching content and released it. Educators were not required to create specialist content, although making content available for release is not a frictionless process, since the material often required reversioning, rights clearance or some form of adaptation. MIT estimates that it costs US$3.5M annually to add to and run their OpenCourseWare site. But nevertheless the initiative didn't rely on individual educators engaging with complicated standards and adopting a new set of practices. Instead, OpenCourseWare built on standard practice by taking existing course materials and releasing these, rather than developing bespoke learning objects.

Following on from the MIT announcement, an OER movement began, with many other universities following suit. These projects were often funded by foundations such as the William and Flora Hewlett foundation, or national initiatives such as the Joint Information Systems Committee (JISC) in the UK.

An appropriate question to ask at this juncture is, why have so many universities sought to make material freely available? A JISC review of the various OER programmes in the UK identified five major motivations (McGill et al. 2013):

- building reputation of individuals or institutions or communities
- improving efficiency, cost and quality of production
- opening access to knowledge
- enhancing pedagogy and the students' learning experience
- building technological momentum

As the authors point out, these motivations are not exclusive and often overlap. Similarly, the Hewlett Foundation (2013) state five motivations for why they fund the OER field:

- radically reduce costs
- deliver greater learning efficiency
- promote continuous improvement of instruction and personalized learning

- encourage translation and localization of content
- offer equal access to knowledge for all

This multitude of motivations is a significant point with regards to the battle for openness. Universities are themselves complex institutions that fulfil a variety of roles, including education, research, centres of innovation (Etzkowitz et al. 2000), public engagement, agents of social change (Brennan, King and Lebeau 2004), curation and preservation of knowledge, and the presence of an independent, trusted voice. So it should not be a surprise that open education should similarly have myriad roles and purposes. This functional complexity will be revisited in the next chapter on MOOCs, as it creates tension for commercial entities, who often require a more succinct goal.

OERs are often gathered together in repositories, and the range of these is impressive. It is almost impossible to quantify OERs by time or projects, since it will vary depending on your definition. For example, should you include online collections from museums? YouTube videos? Slideshare presentations? iTunes U downloads? Even if the focus is solely on university based OER projects then the OpenCourseWare Consortium lists some 260 institutional members, all of whom have a commitment to open education and releasing OERs. MIT has now made over 2,000 courses freely available, and the Open University's OpenLearn site has released over 10,000 hours of learning resources. In terms of usage, 71% of undergraduate students in the US had used OERs, although only one in ten used them all the time (Dahlstrom, Walker and Dziuban 2013), around 50% of educators in the US are aware of OER and 40% use it to supplement teaching material (BCG 2012).

The impact of OER on learning is not always easy to quantify, since there is an element of supplemental use of OERs by formal students. There is ample evidence for the *belief* that OERs improve learning, but this is not the same as actual improvement. If we look for improvement in student satisfaction or performance, there is sometimes a divide between the beliefs of educators and students. For example, 63% of educators agreed that using the OU's OpenLearn resources improves student satisfaction, an opinion shared by 85% of K–12 teachers engaged in 'flipped learning' (a teaching approach where learners engage with online resources at home and use class time for interactivity De Los Arcos 2014). However, just 47% of students indicated that using OpenLearn increased their satisfaction with the learning experience (Perryman, Law and Law 2013).

With regards to performance, 44% of educators agreed that using OpenLearn led to improved student grades, and 63% of K–12 teachers agreed that using free online resources in the flipped classroom contributes to higher test scores.

Stronger evidence can be found when comparison points exist, particularly in relation to the adoption of text-free open resources: the Math Department in Byron High School reported a jump from 29.9 % in 2006 to 73.8% in 2011 in Math mastery, and from an average composite score of 21.2 (on a scale of 36) in 2006 to 24.5 in 2011 in ACT scores (Fulton, 2012). Wiley et al. (2012), however, found that the adoption of open textbooks in substitution for traditional textbooks by twenty middle and high school science teachers (and 3,900 students) over two years did not correlate with a change in student scores (either an increase or fall).

This overview of OERs demonstrates that from the initial steps with learning objects, the open approach to education is beginning to establish itself. The availability and uptake of OERs is now entering the mainstream in education, although evidence of impact is still mixed. One format where OERs are gaining particular traction is that of open access textbooks, which will be addressed in the next section.

Open Textbooks

As the Hewlett definition of OERs sets out, they can include textbooks. The field of open textbooks has proven to be one of the most amenable to the open approach, and provides solid evidence of cost savings, and pedagogical benefits. Indeed, in much of North America, open textbooks have become almost synonymous with OERs. The premise of open textbooks is relatively simple – create electronic versions of standard textbooks that are freely available and can be modified by users. The physical versions of such books are available at a low cost to cover printing, for as little as US$5 (Wiley 2011b). The motivations for doing so are particularly evident in the US, where the cost of textbooks accounts for 26% of a 4-year degree programme (GAO 2005). This creates a strong economic argument for their adoption.

There are a number of projects developing open textbooks, using various models of production. A good example is OpenStax, who have funding from several foundations. They target the subject areas with large national student populations, for example, 'Introductory Statistics', 'Concepts of Biology', 'Introduction to Sociology', etc. The books are co-authored and authors are paid a fee to work on the books, which are peer-reviewed. The electronic versions of these are free, and print versions available at cost. The books are released under a CC-BY license, and educators are encouraged to modify the textbooks to suit their own needs. In terms of adoption, the OpenStax textbooks have been downloaded over 120,000 times and 200 institutions have decided to formally adopt OpenStax materials, leading to an estimated US$3 million savings for students

(Green 2013). Similarly, a report by the Open Course Library (Allen 2013) estimated that OCL had saved students US$5.5 million since its inception, with students saving an average of US$96 per course compared with using traditional textbooks – some 90% reduction over the previous cost, which would equate to US$41.6 million at adoption across the state of Washington. The College of the Canyons has estimated its savings from open textbooks to be in the region of US$400,000 (Daly *et al.* 2013) using a formula based on previous purchasing patterns. It should be noted that these savings are often against projected spending of students, and so claiming them can be contentious, as it assumes students would buy the books.

As well as the financial impact, there may well be an educational one, simply because the costs of textbooks prevent many students from purchasing them. Feldstein et al. (2013) reported that while just 47% of students purchased the paper textbooks, most due to finding them unaffordable, when they switched to open textbooks, 93% of students reported reading the free online textbook.

Perhaps one reason why open textbooks are proving to be a fruitful area for OER implementation is that they readily map onto existing practices. One of the problems that learning objects encountered was that in order for them to be successful they required too many alien or novel practices to be adopted – sharing teaching material, uploading it to repositories, tagging it with metadata, using other people's material in elearning courses, etc. Open textbooks simply require an educator (or institution, state or country) to recommend a different textbook. As long as the quality of this book is deemed to be as good, if not better than the standard text, the cost savings alone become an irresistible driver for their uptake. Choosing between two alternatives of equal educational value, the price becomes a factor, and free is difficult to beat. Other factors, such as open licenses and the ability to modify the textbook, become of interest later. For example OpenStax report that of 1,245 resources, 419 have been modified. This suggests that modifying a textbook is still something of an alien practice for many educators, but one that is growing. This is likely to take time to alter, but the open textbooks example illustrates how starting from a well understood practice can lead to successful OER adoption, and from that initial exposure to openness, other practices will follow.

Issues for OERs

One of the issues that is often raised for OER projects is that of sustainability. Many OER projects have received funding from bodies such as the William and Flora Hewlett Foundation. Producing OER and maintaining large projects with associated staff is not a zero cost activity, and so questions arise about maintaining such projects when the original funding ends.

In a report for OECD in 2007, David Wiley defined sustainability as 'an open educational resource project's ongoing ability to meet its goals' (Wiley 2007b p. 5). Wiley proposed three models of sustainability, which he labelled according to the universities that had deployed them:

- the MIT model – OERs are created and released by a dedicated, centralised, paid project team.
- the USU (Utah State University) model – OERs are created by a hybrid of a centralised team and decentralised staff.
- the Rice model – This is a decentralised model based around a community of contributors.

Economic viability of OERs is significant, because the same questions are now being asked of MOOCs and other open approaches.

Many universities require seed funding, usually from a foundation such as Hewlett or a national body such as the JISC, to establish OER projects, but external project funding is not a long-term solution. At the Open University the OpenLearn project operates on a USU model, and has made OER release part of standard practice. Each new course is required to designate a set of materials to be released, which are then 'scrubbed', formatted and made context independent by a central team and released through the OpenLearn repository. The cost of this additional work is covered by the recruitment value of the open material, which covers its costs in terms of student registrations, i.e., those learners who come to OpenLearn and then go on to sign up for a formal course (Perryman, Law & Law, *2013*).

OERs can be sustainable therefore, but there are some costs involved in initial start-up. An alternative model is provided by the open textbook field, who argue that current costs allocated to purchasing textbooks for colleges can be instead diverted to creating textbooks which are open and free to use.

As well as sustainability, some of the issues that beset learning objects have not been completely overcome by OERs. Reluctance by educators to adopt OERs is still an issue, which can arise from difficulty in finding OERs, the time taken to adapt them and their context (Wiley's reusability paradox) (McGill 2012).

There is still a supply problem, which arises from a cultural issue in teachers sharing material readily, despite growing awareness of OERs. For instance, a survey of teachers in the flipped learning network found that whilst 70% of respondents reported that open licensing is important when using free online resources in their teaching, only 43% of teachers publish the resources they create publicly online and only 5% under a CC license (De Los Arcos, *2014*). However, there is greater awareness of sharing material, and through sites such as iTunes U, Flickr and YouTube, the barriers, both technical and cultural, to sharing content have lowered considerably. We will return to this when we look at open scholarship in Chapter 7.

A Success Story?

The argument of this book is that openness has been a successful approach, and while that is relatively easy to establish for open access publishing, it is less clear with OERs. From the perspective of establishing a movement that has continued to grow over more than a decade, then OERs are a reasonable success story, compared with learning objects, say, or many other educational technology movements. However, they have not completely transformed education or disrupted it to the extent that many hoped for (Kortemeyer 2013). It has taken them over ten years and considerable investment to get to this stage, but they are now entering the global mainstream in education, and the next decade is likely to determine if their usage moves from supplementary to primary position in many forms of education. This timeframe and scale of investment is significant because it gives some indication as to the effort required to make an impact in education. The efficiency and pedagogic benefits of OERs have been apparent since the days of learning objects, but there are considerable barriers to overcome in realising these, including cultural ones such as educator reluctance to reuse other's materials.

This indicates that the effort required to make even a modest impact in the education sector should not be underestimated. Such long-term stories with nuanced outcomes are difficult to relate to a general audience, and the media has a preference for a certain type of narrative, which we shall explore in Chapter 6.

This meant that while OERs were largely overlooked by the mass media, the overnight revolution of MOOCs offered a more palatable story. But given the investment required to transform education, it is debatable whether many companies with venture capitalist backing will be able to wait ten years for their impact to be realised. In his critical analysis of Tim O'Reilly, Morozov (2013) makes a point about the different time scales of the free and open source movements we saw in Chapter 2, which have relevance here:

> Stallman the social reformer could wait for decades until his ethical argument for free software prevailed in the public debate. O'Reilly the savvy businessman had a much shorter timeline: a quick embrace of open source software by the business community guaranteed steady demand for O'Reilly books and events, especially at a time when some analysts were beginning to worry

If one replaces 'free software' with OERs and 'open source software' with MOOCs in Morozov's analysis then a similar pattern is apparent. OERs, largely conceived of as a social good allied to the roles of the university, can afford to take their time to realise their goal, and indeed understand that such change *does* take time. MOOCs, particularly those with venture capital funding, are under pressure to realise more rapid and more dramatic impact. In Chapter 1 one of the reasons for positing the issues in open education as a battle was that of narrative. This need for rapid results to realise commercial targets creates a context where narratives of revolution and disruption are not only desirable, but essential. This is a topic that will be explored in more detail in Chapter 6, but for now it is worth noting the timescale, investment and hard work required by the OER community to realise their long-term goals.

The Battle for OER

If we return to the theme of the book, that openness now faces a battle as to its future direction, then what might be the focus of that battle for OER? One such area might be competition from commercial interests in the OER space. OER has largely been a movement driven from within education, but there are commercial aspects too. The motivation for many universities is not purely altruistic; brand awareness, marketing and student recruitment are also part of the justification for an OER policy. In addition to OERs that are generated by educational institutions, a number of companies use them either as supplementary material to their core product or as their primary offering, and in other cases there is a blurred boundary between commercial and open interests. For example, the Virtual School creates OERs for teachers (in collaboration with the teachers themselves), and releases them under a CC license. It is created and funded by the corporate elearning company Fusion Universal and set up as a social enterprise. The Khan Academy is a not-for-profit organisation that creates and openly shares educational resources in the form of instructional videos. The founder, Salman Khan, was reckoned to be 'the most influential person in educational technology' by *Forbes* (High 2014). The Khan Academy has a reported 6 million visitors a month (Khan Academy 2013), and their approach was very influential on many of the MOOC founders, such as Sebastian Thrun (High 2013), so maybe this claim isn't too exaggerated, at least in terms of media coverage.

A different take on OERs is provided by OpenEd, which is a catalogue of resources, including games and assessment for K–12, many aligned to the US Common Core standard. These are from other creators, such as the Khan Academy, but the service gathers the resources around standards and also offers a Learning Management System and an API for other systems to integrate with the resources. The educational publisher Pearson has launched OpenClass, an online learning platform that is free to use and allows educators to create their own courses by using OERs (either their own or from elsewhere). In this model the provision of OERs is a route through which a learning platform can be marketed.

The OpenClass initiative is interesting because its announcement was met with a good deal of scepticism. Pearson isn't well known for giving content away or being part of the open movement. So a number of commentators wondered what was in it for Pearson to offer a free LMS (learning management system). Kim (2011) suggested they should be 'brutally honest about the threats to a publisher of the shift from paper textbooks to digital content and the need for publishers to not lose control of the sales channel'. While Watters (2011) cautioned that we 'need to question its usage of adjectives like "free" and "open"'. These responses indicate the wariness around commercial providers adopting open approaches, as the suspicion is that this form of open is being used to tie users into their paid for services at a later date or to try and establish a monopoly (although Pearson have stressed that they do not intend to up-sell further content to the OpenClass users).

However, commercial providers offering OERs is not necessarily to the detriment of the OER movement; in many respects it is a welcome and necessary addition to the larger pool of resources. It is only an issue if, as with the case of the green movement, it begins to undermine the core value of openness.

The issues facing OERs are perhaps best encapsulated by a report released in 2014. The National Association of College Stores examined the use of open textbooks created by the Open Course

Library (OCL) project in Washington State (Biemiller 2014). Their findings were discouraging for OER advocates, reporting that 'Of the 98,130 students enrolled in these 42 courses on the 25 campuses, only 2,386 were in sections that used the recommended OCL materials.' The report was somewhat strange, for a number of reasons. Firstly, the research was conducted by college stores, and many users of open, online textbooks would not go via the college stores to acquire these. One might also wonder if college stores are entirely in favour of free, online resources. But even if we ignore methodological concerns and accept the uptake is low, this is revealing about the context within which OERs operate. One might suppose that given the choice between a textbook that costs, say, US$100 and one that is free (or the physical copy is available for US$25), then the latter would prove to be more popular. The reasons the take-up may be lower than expected indicate the areas for the next phase of the OER movement. First amongst these is simply awareness of the resources. Commercial publishers have sophisticated and expensive marketing tools and expertise, and competing with this to simply make lecturers and students aware of the open alternative will be problematic for non-profit organisations. The second issue is less a financial one, and more cultural. Books are recommended by lecturers, many of whom have used the same book for several years and constructed a curriculum around it. To change to an alternative, no matter how good it might be, requires additional effort. While lecturers may care about the cost to students, the cost of textbooks is not borne by them, so there is no direct incentive to switch to free alternatives. This is not to say they don't care, but rather that it is not always a priority for often over-worked faculty. In addition, many universities make a percentage of sales from the campus bookstores, so again there is no strong incentive to reduce costs.

What the OCL report reveals then is that simply creating OERs that are of good quality and freely available may not be sufficient to ensure adoption. There is a long-standing cultural ecosystem surrounding the current use of textbooks, and the new open versions need to address all the different elements of this to bring success.

Conclusions

In the different categories of open education, OERs can be seen as occupying a middle ground, intersecting with open access, through open textbooks, and MOOCs, which can be seen as a subset of OERs. The OER field is constituted of a mixture of universities, national agencies, not-for-profit organisations and commercial interests. While there are some reservations about the intentions of the commercial players, the combination of OER providers represents a healthy mixture of different interests. The principles of OER are well established; they benefit from a fairly clear definition which foregrounds the importance of reuse and open licenses. Therefore, any entrants and participants in the field are obliged to behave in an open manner to a large extent. This may be a result of the altruistic roots of the movement and the time it had to establish itself, with educational providers and not-for-profits being the main drivers. As a consequence, educational establishments have stayed largely prominent in the field.

In terms of impact, OERs have realised success in terms of the number of resources and people accessing those, although some have criticised them for not having a greater impact on everyday practice; for example, Kortemeyer (2013) bemoans that 'OERs have not noticeably disrupted the traditional business model of higher education or affected daily teaching approaches at most institutions.' However, the impact can be seen in a number of different aspects. The OER Research Hub (2013) set out eleven hypotheses which represented many of the key beliefs propounded regarding OERs:

1. Use of OER leads to improvement in student performance and satisfaction.
2. The open aspect of OER creates different usage and adoption patterns than other online resources.
3. Open education models lead to more equitable access to education, serving a broader base of learners than traditional education.
4. Use of OER is an effective method for improving retention for at-risk students.
5. Use of OER leads to critical reflection by educators, with evidence of improvement in their practice.
6. OER adoption at an institutional level leads to financial benefits for students and/or institutions.
7. Informal learners use a variety of indicators when selecting OER.
8. Informal learners adopt a variety of techniques to compensate for the lack of formal support, which can be supported in open courses.
9. Open education acts as a bridge to formal education, and is complementary, not competitive, with it.
10. Participation in OER pilots and programs leads to policy change at the institutional level.
11. Informal means of assessment are motivators to learning with OER.

These beliefs would often be stated as obvious, undeniably true or based on anecdote, but rarely backed up by evidence. The OER movement has gained sufficient momentum to investigate these more fully now, and the evidence for OER impact can be found at the Impact Map (OER Research Hub 2014). In general, evidence was found to support the hypotheses, although it was still equivocal and nuanced for some. This pattern of initial belief-driven promotion followed by objective evaluation is a necessary one to pursue in new fields. As we saw in Chapter 2, the combination of digital resources and the internet has created new possibilities which don't have a precedent to draw upon. Therefore, for new fields such as OERs to reach a mature state when critical evaluation is possible, an initial phase characterised by experimentation and often evangelism is required.

OERs can be put forward as a success story for open education – they have had a positive impact for learners, they have developed sustainable models of operation, there is a thriving global community, the open aspect has been retained and there is a resonance with the social function of education, all wrapped up in a modern, 21st century, digital approach. If we revisit the principles of openness listed in Chapter 2, then we can see that OERs fare well against them:

- Freedom to reuse – open licences are part of the OER definition
- Open access – a defining characteristic
- Free cost – usually, although some commercial providers operate a 'freemium' model, whereby some content is free and some is paid for
- Easy use – generally they are, although modifying OER content can require specialist skills
- Digital, networked content – yes, although note previous point about awareness of OERs

- Social, community based approaches – a good OER community exists, and for many specific projects the open approach has been key to building communities
- Ethical arguments for openness – these have formed the basis for most OER projects
- Openness as efficient model – increasingly seen with the open textbook approach

Given this, it is worth asking then why this success story is not as widely reported in the popular press as that of MOOCs? Why would one educational technology blogger proclaim that MOOCs had led to 'more action in 1 year than [the] last 1,000 years'? (Clark 2013). The Hewlett Foundation (*2013*, pg. 16) felt moved to point out that 'we are seeing a lot of confusion in the market about the terms "Open" and "OER". One example is the rise of massive online open courses (MOOCs), which have spurred a great deal of attention for the movement.' Just what *is* it about MOOCs that has caused so much attention in the popular media, while OERs have been largely ignored? Answering this question will reveal much about open education and the tensions within and is the subject of the next chapter.

CHAPTER 5

MOOCs

Beware of the man who works hard to learn something, learns it, and finds himself no wiser than before. He is full of murderous resentment of people who are ignorant without having come by their ignorance the hard way.

—Kurt Vonnegut

Introduction

Having looked at a long established practice of open access publishing in Chapter 3 and a relatively stable approach of OERs in Chapter 4, this chapter will consider the rapid and rather volatile world of MOOCs. No subject in educational technology in recent years has generated as much excitement amongst educational entrepreneurs and angst amongst established academics as MOOCs. If open access represents the clearest case for the argument that openness has been successful, then MOOCs are probably the best example of the second strand of this – that the battle for the future direction is now occurring.

It was MOOCs after all, and not OERs, open access or open scholarship, that caused veteran elearning expert Tony Bates (2014) to despair, 'I can't express adequately just how pissed off I am about MOOCs – not the concept, but all the hubris and nonsense that's been talked and written about them. At a personal level, it was as if 45 years of work was for nothing.' Why should this be so? What is it about MOOCs that causes despair and excitement in equal measure? This will be the subject of the next two chapters, concentrating first on MOOCs themselves, and then on the media interest around them in the Chapter 6. MOOCs can stand as a microcosm of the issues in open education, because it is with open courses that they are brought into sharpest relief.

This rapid growth of MOOCs can be demonstrated by comparing their internet interest with that of OERs. A simple use of Google Trends reveals how interest in MOOCs has grown, comparative to OERs (see **Figure 4**).

While OERs have had steady growth since 2009, indicating an increased awareness, MOOCs arrive seemingly from nowhere in late 2012 and rapidly overtake OERs. This plot emphasises the point made at the end of the previous chapter regarding the sudden media interest in MOOCs. However, to put it in perspective, we can also plot MOOCs against a subject that has wider public awareness. Zuckerman (2012) jokingly suggests using the US celebrity Kim Kardashian to act as an indicative measure of internet attention. **Figure 5** shows this comparison, and because Google Trends normalises the Y-scale so that it is showing relative interest rather than absolute number of searches, the rather sobering evidence is that in this plot, MOOCs don't even register.

There are two interesting aspects of MOOCs from the perspective of the battle for open. The first is what they are, the opportunities and threats they pose and the type of openness they afford. The second is the media interest in them and why they find resonance with a certain type of narrative. This chapter will deal with the first of these, looking at the history, benefits,

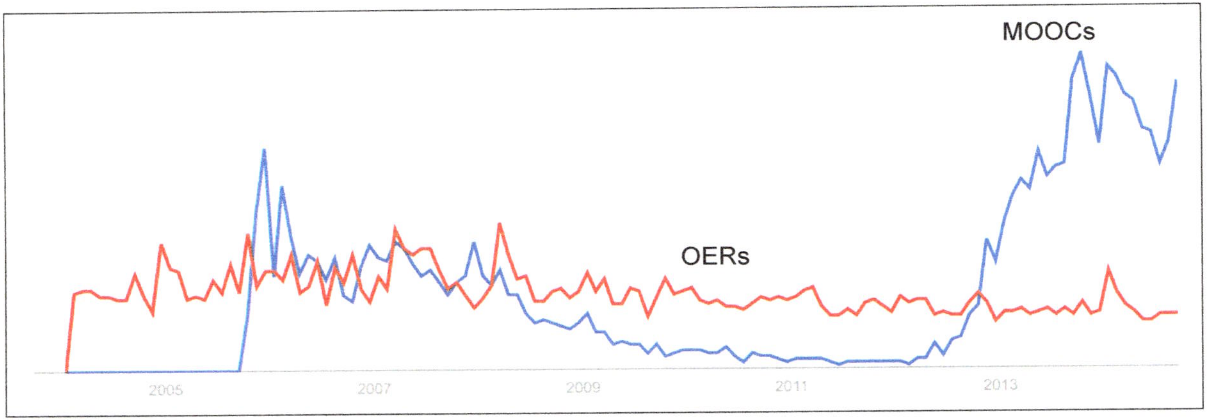

Figure 4: Google Trends plot of relative interest in MOOCs and OERs.

Source: Google Trends http://www.google.com/trends/explore#q=moocs%2C%20OERs&cmpt=q. (7th September 2014)

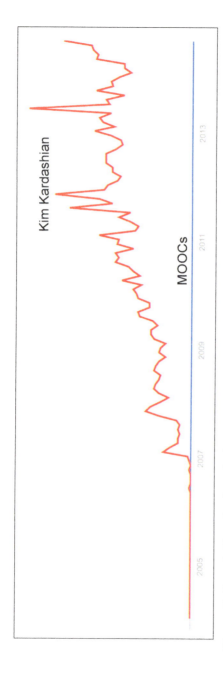

Figure 5: Google Trends plot of relative interest in MOOCs vs. Kim Kardashian

Source: Google Trends http://www.google.com/trends/explore#q=moocs%2C%20Kardashian&cmpt=q. (7th September 2014)

commercialisation and pedagogy of MOOCs. The next chapter will examine the second issue, that of narrative, in detail.

MOOC Background

MOOCs are a topic where a number of people can lay claim to being the instigator. What counts as a MOOC is open to interpretation. People had released content previously, either as part of the OER movement or independently, and this could be in the form of a whole course. However, there was a coalescence of interest around running open courses from a number of people associated with the open education movement. David Wiley ran a campus based course in 2007 and made it open to anyone online to participate, as did Alec Couros, operating an 'open boundary' course. However, the title of founder is often given to Connectivism and Connective Knowledge (CCK08), run by George Siemens and Stephen Downes, in 2008. It was commentary on this course that gave rise to the term MOOC, jointly attributed to Dave Cormier and Bryan Alexander.

There are familiar names in this list of early MOOC providers because MOOCs can be seen as a logical extension of the open education movement. What characterised these early MOOCs was an interest in the possibilities that being open and networked offered. The subject matter of these early courses was related to the mode of presentation, so courses were in topics such as open education, digital identity or networked pedagogy. As with early elearning courses, which would often be about the subject of elearning itself, these early stages of experimentation focused on subjects where the medium was the message. But as with elearning, this soon broadened out to encompass all topics.

Another characteristic of these early MOOCs was that they were associated with individuals, not institutions. They were seen as George and Stephen's course, rather than a Stanford or MIT course. This meant that they were experimental in terms of technology, both by necessity and design. These MOOCs used a combination of open technologies, such as WordPress and Twitter, some institutional hosting through tools such as Moodle, and even some self-created tools such as Stephen Downes's gRSShopper. Learning to use these tools and to make connections across the open internet was seen as a key aim for these early MOOCs.

Then in 2011, MOOCs took a very different turn when Sebastian Thrun launched the Stanford Artificial Intelligence course, with over 120,000 enrolled learners. This attracted much attention from the media and venture capitalists. With the cost of formal education soaring, the idea that you could take courses from the top universities for free seemed irresistible. Harvard and MIT created EdX, Coursera was launched by Daphne Koller and Andrew Ng with venture capital funding and Thrun founded Udacity. The year 2012 was deemed 'Year of the MOOC' by the *New York Times* (Pappano 2012) as most major US universities signed up to one or other of the main providers, or launched their own courses. MOOC mania was not restricted to North America: in the UK the OU launched FutureLearn in 2013; in Germany it was iVersity; and in Australia, Open2Study. Coursera is the most prominent of the MOOC providers, and it has over 500 courses from 107 universities and over 5 million learners enrolled (Protalinski 2013). The pace of uptake, hype and development seemed breathless in comparison with most educational projects.

These new MOOCs were very different from the early ones pioneered by the open education movement. They tended to be institutional, based on a proprietary platform and driven by a strongly instructivist pedagogy. Whereas the initial MOOCs had emphasised the importance of networking, many new MOOCs were focused on video instruction and automatic assessment. The distinction was made between cMOOCs for the early, connectivist type MOOCs and xMOOCs for the new, didactic models (Siemens 2012).

Before we examine the impact of this commercial aspect on the nature of openness in MOOCs, it is worth considering some of the positive aspects of the rapid increase in profile for open education and elearning in general. For many educational technologists who had strived for years to get fellow academics or senior managers interested in different aspects of open education, MOOCs provided a means of getting attention and funding. As Siemens (2014) puts it, 'if education was grunge, MOOCs were its Nirvana', the breakthrough act that gained attention. It might be incorrect to cast the global education movement as a fringe movement such as grunge rock, but MOOCs certainly accelerated the attention and interest in open education.

Such increased profile can be both a blessing and a curse, particularly when it follows on the back of hype about revolution in higher education. But even setting aside the possibly dubious benefits of suddenly becoming the popular child in class, MOOCs are important because they raise a number of issues for educators, and – crucial to the theme of this book – these issues arise directly as a result of the open nature of MOOCs. In the following section, three of these are addressed. These are not the only issues raised by MOOCs, nor is this an exhaustive coverage of them – course design and pedagogy could form a book in itself. The intention here is to illustrate how the open nature of MOOCs causes fundamental questions to be asked about accepted education practice.

MOOCs and Quality

The first such issue is that of quality and how it is measured. Formal higher education has developed a set of quality measures based on a specific relationship between the education provider and the student. That relationship is fundamentally altered in a MOOC, and so these existing measures are not applicable.

Let us consider why we measure quality. Largely it is to verify that aims and intentions have been met. The aims of the institution may be to have a sufficient number of students, for them to stay with and pass the course, and for the institution's reputation to be upheld. The educator in charge of the course may have similar aims, along with those of a professional interest in exploring the possibilities afforded by MOOCs. The student will have the aims of learning what they set out to, passing the course, enjoying the experience and gaining useful skills.

We therefore develop quality measures and procedures that monitor these intentions. These could be student completion rates, student satisfaction scores, external assessment of course content, checks against external benchmarks, etc. In a MOOC many of these intentions are altered, either radically or subtly. At the moment it's not entirely clear what the intentions of institutions are in relation to MOOCs – is it to attract more formal students, to provide a public good, to make money? In this early stage it might be a confused mixture of all of these, combined with a need to appear to be doing something. For educators, the intention might be experimentation with curriculum or pedagogy, improvement of their personal reputation or personal development.

A more interesting difference arises if the intentions of the learner are considered. While some of the original aims may remain, for instance, it may help in career development, others are exaggerated or absent. The need to pass the course, for instance, is drastically reduced, because progress on to subsequent courses is not dependent on it, and most importantly, because there is no financial commitment and the personal interest in learning is heightened. In conventional courses there will be a wide range of different types of learner, but in MOOCs, the presence of what are termed 'leisure learners' is much higher than normal. They're nearly all leisure learners – they don't have to do this after all, it's something that is competing with leisure pursuits. A whole new class of learners exist in MOOCs that you rarely see in formal education. These are what we might term drive-by learners (after Groom's 2011 'drive-by assignments'). These are learners who are signing up because they can. It costs nothing to sign up; they can take a look, see if they like anything and move on. They may dip in and out over the course, taking bits they find engaging, or they may not even turn up at all. In formal education the financial and emotional commitment is much higher, making drive-by learners very rare. Kizilcec, Piech and Schneider (2013) used analytics to differentiate four types of MOOC learners: completing, auditing, disengaging and sampling. Although a comparison of these four types with formal learners has not been completed, one could assume that the commitments required to continue in formal education reduces the likelihood of sampling and auditing students, with the emphasis on completing.

If we consider these new types of learners and their intentions, then the existing quality measures don't map across satisfactorily. For instance, very few of these learners have course completion as a major goal. And progression on to other courses is not yet a metric in a pick-and-choose world, although we will undoubtedly see increasing pressures to make MOOC learners persist with a particular brand of MOOC provider, just as we see this with computer or phone providers. With such a broad range of learners, MOOCs find themselves up against a tough comparison with formal education. To use Weinberger's (2007) phrase, higher education 'filters on the way in', whereas MOOCs 'filter on the way out'. The quality measures are therefore very different. Student satisfaction rates for a system that has completely open enrolment and filters on the way out are unlikely to compare favourably with a very different system where there has been a filtering already. Filtering on the way out and operating in the open does, however, allow for new types of quality measures. These could be altmetrics-type measures (what kind of 'buzz' does it create, what is the public reaction of participants) or analytics (how many people come back, what is the dwell time, bounce rate, etc.). But the comparisons should be with other MOOCs, not with formal education. Quality, and what is measured, is therefore just one example of established practices that the attention on MOOCs should make us reconsider.

MOOCs and Cost

A second issue that MOOCs raise for formal education is that they force an examination of the costs associated with teaching. Estimates of how much it takes to produce a MOOC vary, with Udacity budgeting US$200,000, EdX US$250,000 (DeJong 2013) and University of North Carolina estimating US$150,000 for their Coursera MOOC (Goldstein 2013). Once created, the idea is that they can be run at next to no cost, although this will depend on how closely involved the lead academic is in each presentation. Clearly if you are not charging fees for people to study on a course, then its presentation costs need to be low if it is to be a sustainable model. As we saw with OERs, there are different models of sustainability, and seed funding is often required, but eventually such approaches need to stand on their own.

The costs of elearning in general (not MOOCs) has been analysed by a number of researchers (e.g. Bates 1995, Weller 2004). Costs can be divided into production, i.e., those costs associated with creating the course material and any associated resources, rights, etc., and presentation costs, those associated with the delivery of the course. Generally the production costs are fixed, particularly in elearning, so they don't vary with the number of students, while presentation costs are variable, so they increase with the number of students. The key difference for MOOCs is that in order to achieve the scale they desire, while remaining free to study, this model is not viable. Presentation costs for MOOCs need to be close to zero.

The basic model of MOOCs is that of unsupported learning; in cMOOCs this support is replaced by a peer network, in xMOOCs, by automatic feedback. At the Open University, ratios for course production and presentation costs over five presentations, averaged across disciplines, are estimated to be about 1:3. That is, the presentation costs are the most expensive element, once the initial production costs have been invested. This is largely made up of salaries paid to part-time tutors to support students, but also other generic and specific student support services, e.g. support for students with disabilities, pastoral support, helpdesk costs, running regional centres, etc. This illustrates that by far the biggest cost is that of tuition. Paying people to support learners is the costly part of education.

In order for MOOCs to be viable they need to remove much of these presentation costs. The question that MOOCs make higher education ask of itself is, what value is this set of costs to learners? Many of the services it represents are the key to long-term success for learners. The need for these may not be evenly distributed, though. Some learners hardly ever avail themselves of these, don't require tuition and do very well studying on their own. Other learners require a lot of support for various reasons and probably have more than their 'fair' share of these services (i.e., more than they've actually paid for). And most are in the middle; they make use of them sometimes, depending on circumstances.

For distance education in particular, this first group, the confident, independent learners will probably cope well with MOOCs. They probably represent the 10% or so who complete MOOCs. Then there are some for whom no amount of support can help them through, either study isn't for them or this is the wrong time. But sitting in the middle is a substantial group who need varying levels of support to 'survive' a protracted course of study.

But that doesn't necessarily mean that universities shouldn't look at ways of reducing the cost of presentation. This highlights the dilemma for universities – many students may not think they need these services, but they are essential for long-term success. It's akin to a universal credit, such as a state pension. Some need it more than others, but if you remove the principle of all paying into it, then it becomes prohibitively expensive for those who do need it. So the question that MOOCs make both universities and students address is – how much do we value support? It's a profound question for the future direction of education.

MOOCs and Course Design

The third and final issue we will consider relates to course design. As mentioned in Chapter 1, being open creates a number of different opportunities for pedagogy. There are many different possibilities and motivations for being open, and as mentioned earlier, open pedagogy would make a good book subject on its own. This section will focus on just one aspect, to again illustrate how the open nature of MOOCs raises different issues which then have a consequent impact on standard educational practice.

One of the oft-cited problems with MOOCs is their low completion rate. Some argue that to talk of completion rates in MOOCs is to miss their point. Downes (2014) has commented, 'Nobody ever complained that newspapers have low completion rates.' Learners take what they want from a MOOC in the same way that readers take what they want from a newspaper. Others state that MOOCs can't really back up their revolutionary claims when only about 10% of learners complete a MOOC (Lewin 2013).

Jordan and Weller (2013a) have done some work plotting completion rates taking the various sources of publicly available data. The average completion rate (and there are different ways of defining completion) was 12.6%. A study by the University of Pennsylvania found lower completion rates of around 4% (Perna et al. 2013). **Figure 6** plots the attrition rates of active users, i.e., those that come into the course and do something such as watching a video, across disciplines:

The pattern in Figure 6 is very consistent across all disciplines. Given this fairly robust pattern of behaviour, there are two course design responses.

Design for Retention

The first response is to say that completion *is* a desired metric. There may be courses where it is desirable that as many people as possible complete. For example, a remedial maths course will require learners to complete a majority of the topics. The Bridge2Success project used a MOOC-like approach to aid

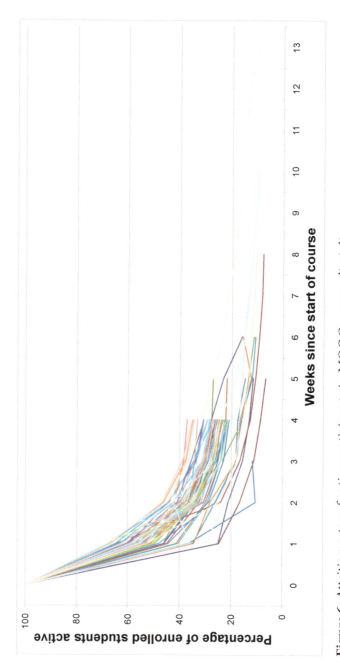

Figure 6: Attrition rates of active participants in MOOCs across disciplines. *Source:* Jordan and Weller 2013a. Published under a CC-BY license.

learners with maths so they could gain a place on an employment program, so completion was very important (Pitt et al. 2013).

In this case the course design needs to address the 'problem' of drop-out rates. There might be a number of ways of attempting this: by adding in more feedback, using badges to motivate people, creating support structures, supplementing with face-to-face study groups, breaking longer courses into shorter ones, etc.

Design for Selection

The second design approach is to decide that completion *isn't* an important metric. The course designer accepts the MOOC attrition rates in **Figure 7** and designs the experience with that in mind.

In this design approach the designer might break away from the linear course model, to allow people to engage in the 'newspaper' type selection that Downes refers to. A course might be structured around themes, for instance, and each one around largely independent activities. In this case course completion really doesn't matter, since learners take what they want.

As a slight aside, it is likely that MOOC completion rates are being defined in such a way that gives them a low output compared with formal education, largely because the manner in which enrolment is defined is so broad. In formal education there are different ways of defining who has enrolled on a course, but it usually allows a cooling-off period. Students are not counted as being enrolled if they drop out in the first two weeks or fail to turn up at all. So, taking MOOC enrolment figures to be the number who signed up for a MOOC even if they never come into it is always going to give harsh figures. A better figure might be the number of students active after 1 week. This is the baseline figure as those are the students who have actually started the course.

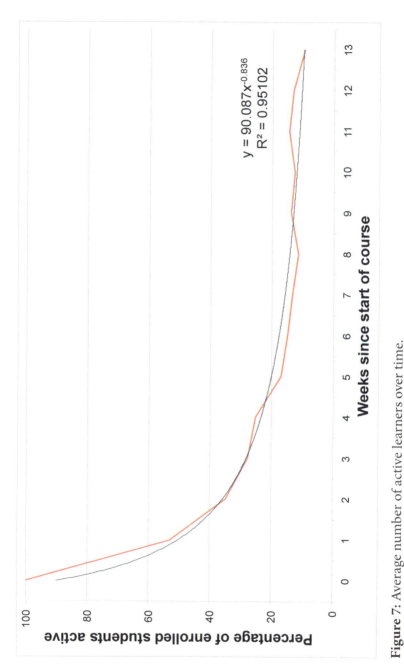

Figure 7: Average number of active learners over time.

Source: Jordan and Weller 2013b. Published under a CC-BY license.

Another graph Jordan and Weller (2013b) plotted showed the average number of students active across weeks (**Figure** 7), starting with the initial enrolment figures.

At the end of week 1, there are about 55% of students still active from the initial registration point. Many of those who registered will not even have come into the course once, so it is misleading to say they have dropped out. If this 55% figure is taken as the actual enrolment statistic as our starting figure, then the average completion rate rises to around 23%. With open entry learners on an unsupported course, this figure might not be as catastrophic as the numbers often quoted. There is a flip side to redefining completion rates in this way, in that it drastically reduces the impressive enrolment figures used to justify MOOC investments.

What this example and the preceding two demonstrate is that there are beneficial, or at least significant, issues raised for formal education by MOOCs. This is one of the strengths of openness – it causes us to examine assumptions in standard practice, which can be improved or altered. How educators design, cost and assess the quality of all courses, not just open ones, becomes altered by digital, networked applications, but it is the addition of the catalyst of openness that really accelerates the changes and possibilities. It is this positive impact of MOOCs that I want to focus on before examining their possible downsides. The next section will examine how MOOCs could relate to higher education and perform a complementary function.

MOOCs as Complement to Formal Education

Much of the hype around MOOCs has positioned them as being in competition to formal education. While this adversarial framing may make good sense in terms of a media narrative, as we will see in the next chapter, it underplays both the actual impact of MOOCs and the adaptability of education. An alternative perspective is to view MOOCs as being similar to OERs, and complementary to formal education. Five such possible functions for MOOCs are set out below.

Open up a portion of courses – An online (or blended) course could be structured so that a portion of it functions as a standalone MOOC. This allows students to see if it's the type of course they want to study, to make connections and experience studying. This type of trialling has been found to be quite significant with OERs (e.g. Perryman, Law and Law 2013). It has several benefits for the institution and the learner. Firstly, it acts as a shop window, so it can increase student recruitment. Secondly, it can increase student retention, since those learners who will struggle can find this out for free and either take a different subject, study at a different level or take preparatory material. Thirdly it can widen participation, reaching audiences that the institution may have struggled to reach before. However, it should also be said that without support, the experience may be negative for some students and put them off from studying further.

Open boundary courses – As we have already encountered, some courses that have a campus based cohort can be made open to all. The digital storytelling course DS106 and the photography course Phonar are good examples of such courses. As well as the advantages set out above, this has particular benefits in certain subject areas. Photography is one such area where exposure to a wider audience, including professionals and experienced hobbyists, is beneficial. But for all students there is a benefit in developing a network of peers beyond their immediate cohort.

MOOC collaboration – Institutions could collaborate on MOOCs which are useful for a range of their students. The same logic that underpinned learning objects comes into play here: Why teach the same subject at several places, when one high-quality MOOC can be created for all students to take that is recognised by all participating institutions?

MOOC recognition – By formally recognising certain MOOCs, it is possible that some institutions could shorten some of the courses they offer. For example, a learner could demonstrate that they have successfully completed a determined number of MOOCs, then they could enter an undergraduate degree in the second year and complete in two years. For the students it means fees are reduced by at least a third, which might make degree study more attractive. For campus universities they are selling the 'campus experience' more, without it being as prohibitively expensive. There would be reservations about developing some higher level, graduate skills with this approach, but it is feasible that a few institutions might adopt it to differentiate themselves.

Curriculum experimentation and expansion – Formal online courses are an increasingly large investment, which means course approval becomes more rigorous. The demands placed on a formal course are lessened for a MOOC (although they do not disappear), which allows for experimentation. And because MOOCs appeal to a global audience, what may not be a viable course for a campus, fee paying constituency may well be viable to a global community of informal learners. The result is that curriculum experimentation becomes less risky. It also means institutions can offer a broader curriculum, because they can offer their own curriculum but also recognise MOOCs from others. For example, 'Hydro-engineering and Russian' may be offered by a university that covers the engineering element, while Russian language is delivered via third-party MOOCs which are accredited and supported by the host university.

These possible scenarios illustrate how MOOCs could benefit formal education and operate alongside it in a sustainable model. However, much of the recent coverage of MOOCs has not focused on these possibilities, and instead has stressed the concept of MOOC as a replacement for university. This is partly a function of the commercial nature of many MOOC entrants, and it is this aspect that will be explored next.

The Commercialisation of MOOCs

Soon after Sebastian Thrun's MOOC caught the attention of the media, a number of commercial MOOC providers were established with venture capital funding. The most significant of these were Thrun's own Udacity and another Stanford based start-up, Coursera, led by Daphne Koller and Andrew Ng. After an initial investment of $22 million, Coursera gained a further $43 million in 2013 (Kolowich 2013a).

The business model of MOOC providers is not always clear. Coursera have stated that they have earned US$1 million in revenue through selling certificates of completion, which cost between US$30 and US$100 (Heussner 2013). They also announced an employee matching service, Careers Service, whereby employers could pay a fee to be matched with the best performing MOOC students (Young 2012). These elements of headhunting and certification were combined by creating a paid-for 'Signature Track' model, whereby students pay a fee to have verifiable identity, records and certification (Coursera 2013a). In May 2013 Coursera also announced that they were partnering with 10 campus universities to offer campus based MOOCs (Coursera 2013b), where students on campus could take a MOOC with local support. This positioned them as an elearning courseware provider, which Mike Caulfield (2013) had suggested was the intention all along.

In the meantime Sebastian Thrun announced that Udacity were close to finding the 'magic formula' for education (Carr 2013). Then in an interview in November 2013, driven by the completion rates outlined above, he announced that Udacity had a 'lousy product' and they were repositioning themselves to provide corporate training (Chafkin 2013). Such a pivot drew a considerable degree of comment and derision given the bold claims Thrun had made previously, with Siemens (2013) perhaps summing it up most succinctly: 'Make no mistake – this is a failure of Udacity and Sebastian Thrun. This is not a failure of open education, learning at scale, online learning, or MOOCs. Thrun tied his fate too early to VC funding. As a result, Udacity is now driven by revenue pursuits, not innovation.'

It is Siemens's last point that is worth pursuing in the context of MOOCs – the influence of venture capital funding. We should not be surprised that Coursera have attempted a range of business models, such an approach is not unusual with internet start-ups. It does suggest, however, that they are not entirely sure what the role of MOOCs is. Koller (2012) has promoted the democratisation of learning that MOOCs and Coursera offer as a social good, and their figures are impressive, with over 17 million enrolments by September 2013 (Coursera 2013c) – although this number should be treated with caution regarding what constitutes an enrolment, as mentioned previously. For comparison, there are only 2,300,000 students in higher education in the whole of the UK (HESA 2013). It might seem churlish therefore to criticise Coursera and other MOOC providers for providing access to free education. This section will not address issues such as pedagogy, which some have levelled as a criticism against MOOCs. While some of these accusations may be valid, they often betray either a snobbishness regarding all online learning or an over-estimation of the variety and face to face contact that many students experience.

Instead the focus here will be on the open aspect of MOOCs. Although early findings (Kolowich 2013b) suggest that successful learners tend to be experienced learners with existing degrees, it may well be that given time and increased familiarity with MOOCs, Koller may be justified in her vision about the democratisation of learning. However, it is unlikely that such an altruistic goal is the intention of the venture capitalists who have invested $85 million in Coursera. As MOOC companies have shifted their models to try and recoup these costs, they have moved further away from an open model: their contents are not openly licensed, so they cannot be reused by others; enrolment is often restricted to limited periods, so content cannot be accessed without enrolling; and many MOOC providers are limiting the universities they partner with to elite institutions. The Signature Track model of Coursera may be cheap compared with formal education, but it is not an open model, nor is the blended learning, campus based delivery. Udacity's transformation to a corporate elearning company demonstrates how quickly this shift from global provider of open education can occur if it is not founded in principles of openness. There has been a precedent for the Udacity move in FlatWorld Knowledge. FlatWorld was set up as an open access textbook publisher that allowed educators to modify the free online version and sold the physical product for a set price. In 2012 they announced that they were dropping free access to textbooks (Howard 2012), although they would remain an 'affordable solution'. The reason behind this was that their open business model simply wasn't generating sufficient revenue. Affordable textbooks are to be welcomed, but that is a very different entity from an open textbook. As Siemens suggests, close alliance to revenue funding will come to dominate the concerns of start-ups, and openness is usually the first casualty when this happens. Given the costs of creating a MOOC, and the return that universities will start requiring for the investment of their staff, it is debatable whether MOOCs can be sustainable as a stand-alone business. As with OERs, they may be sustainable as an adjunct to existing university practice or for national agencies, charities and professional bodies who have an interest in engaging learners. Unless they are rooted in openness, however, it is unlikely that this will remain a central tenet of their identity. It may well be that MOOC providers transform themselves into low-cost education alternatives by offering a combination of quite sophisticated unsupported courses and automatic assessment. This would have a profound impact on access to education and higher education itself, but it would be a different proposition to their original 'open as in free' model, and it would have more in common with the open entry model of distance education personified by open universities. Whether elite universities would continue to subsidise a low-cost provider through provision of courses then becomes questionable, once the open aspect has been removed.

Conclusions

MOOCs didn't appear overnight from nowhere, although one might be forgiven for thinking so from the coverage they received. **Figure 8** from Yuan and Powell (2013) provides a clear indication of the contributing influences for MOOCs.

While some MOOC providers, such as the Harvard and MIT founded EdX, can be seen as part of a continuum with OERs, others have developed along commercial lines. To learners on

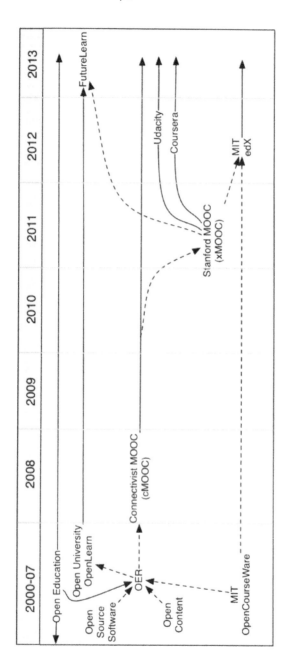

Figure 8: MOOCs and Open Education Timeline.
Source: Yuan & Powell 2013. Published under a CC-BY license.

MOOCs, these ideological differences may not have much of an impact – a Coursera MOOC does not feel radically distinct from an EdX one. As we have seen, though, they may have longer-term implications on the directions that MOOCs take.

The initial MOOCs were largely experimental, explicitly designed to take advantage of the possibilities that being open and networked offered. Openness was thus a key component in their design. As MOOCs became associated more with institutions, they acquired what we might term a 'brand burden'. If MOOCs are to be seen as a global shop window, then their identity becomes closer to that of broadcast rather than network, with high-value production quality. Any failure of a MOOC can lead to considerable negative publicity for the institution, as the example of the Georgia Tech Coursera offering on Fundamentals of Online Education demonstrated (Kolowich 2013c). This course had problems with students using Google Docs to register and had to be suspended, mainly as a result of the scale of users. This shift from acceptable experimentation to part of the institution's communications policy may have benefits in terms of sustainability, as MOOCs can be costed relative to the marketing benefit they gain, which is a model understood by universities. It may however have some negatives such as:

- MOOCs become prohibitively expensive – A good MOOC requires such high-end production that it is not economically viable given the low return.
- Only elite institutions offer MOOCs – Given the expense, only those institutions who have the money or the skills to produce broadcast-quality content will provide them.
- MOOCs become pedagogically conservative – Part of the problem with the Georgia Tech course was that

it was experimenting with a new approach, and if the cost of failure is too high then it becomes better not to attempt anything risky or innovative.

- Fear of MOOC failure becomes a barrier to adoption – Public failure can lead to damage for an individual's and an institution's reputation, so many will consider the risk too great.

In a relatively short space of time, MOOCs would have moved from being a means that allow educators to experiment with technology and pedagogy to another form of broadcast controlled by a few.

This loss of experimentation may also arise as a result of there being a few dominant MOOC providers. Instead of discovering new models of open education, running a MOOC on the Coursera (or EdX or FutureLearn) platform becomes seen as the way to run a MOOC. Diversity in the market is undesirable for commercial providers; they want to become the Microsoft or Google of MOOCs, since that leads to the best revenue. Indeed, becoming the dominant provider may be the only route to high revenue returns in the MOOC field. In the opening chapter I argued that the tensions in open education could be deemed a battle, because there was real value associated with being a victor. A loss of experimentation and market dominance for open courses would be an example of one such outcome.

This perceived loss of control over the platform for open courses has led to a 'Reclaim Open' initiative from MIT and UC Irvine. The Reclaim Open (2013) site bemoans that 'recent high-profile forays into online learning for higher education seem to replicate a traditional lecture-based, course-based model of campus instruction, instead of embracing the peer-to-peer connected nature of the web.' The site promises that 'Reclaim Open

Learning intervenes in this debate by supporting and showcasing innovation that brings together the best of truly open, online and networked learning in the wilds of the Internet.' This can be viewed as a counter-movement to the growing dominance of certain models of MOOCs, which their technology platforms come to embody. The Reclaim Open initiative views engagement with various forms of technology as a route through which educators can take ownership of what it means to be open. Whether one supports Reclaim Open or not, their existence is an indication of the stage we are in for the battle for open, and suggests that ownership of the term is slipping, or has slipped, away. One does not see a 'reclaim exams' or 'reclaim libraries' movement.

If the analysis performed at the end of the last chapter for OERs against the open principles from Chapter 2 is repeated for MOOCs, this reveals some of the reasons for this underlying disquiet about MOOCs:

- Freedom to reuse – MOOC contents are not usually openly licensed, so they cannot be reused in different contexts (some providers have started to use CC licences now)
- Open access – MOOCs are open to all to sign up
- Free cost – this has been the main focus of MOOCs
- Easy use – the MOOC platforms have developed easy-to-use interfaces, although as noted above, the completion rates for this type of learning are low
- Digital, networked content – although MOOCs are obviously online and digital, they are often not fully networked, in that they can exist within a closed platform
- Social, community based approaches – some MOOCs are based around a very community-driven approach,

whereas others are more instructivist and individual paced
- Ethical arguments for openness – the democratisation of learning has been made as an ethical argument for MOOCs, but less on openness itself
- Openness as efficient model – apart from some cMOOCs, MOOCs are not usually developed in the open; instead they tend to be developed as proprietary products from within universities

This is not to discount the impact that companies such as Udacity and Coursera have had. They have raised the profile of elearning and open education considerably and innovated on technological fronts at a much more rapid pace than universities manage. The presence of commercial interests in the field can create a healthy mix of competition, innovation and different perspectives. For learners who are studying free courses the reservations universities and academics have regarding MOOCs may seem like an inevitable case of turkeys not voting for Christmas. However, it would be to the detriment of learners in the long term if one MOOC platform came to dominate or if, having undermined many higher education establishments, MOOCs then began to charge for courses.

Part of the reluctance (or resentment even) regarding MOOCs has been less focused on the actual concept or the providers, but rather as a reaction to the hyperbole and media flurry that has accompanied them. It is important to separate these two aspects out as the inevitable backlash sets in. This is in response to the exaggerated promise made for MOOCs rather than the more nuanced reality they may offer. Examining the nature of this narrative will reveal much regarding the battle for open, and this is the subject of the next chapter.

CHAPTER 6

Education Is Broken and the Silicon Valley Narrative

Revolutions are nipped in the bud or else succeed too quickly. Passion is quickly exhausted.

—Henry Miller

Introduction

In the previous chapter the rise of MOOCs was plotted, and possible opportunities and reservations about them explored. Unlike almost any other educational development, MOOCs have attracted considerable media interest. In this chapter we will explore the underlying reasons for this. In Chapter 1, I argued that the battle for open was in part a battle for narrative, an argument that will be explored in this chapter. Although much of this chapter will focus on MOOCs, as they provide the most ready example of the conflation of education, technology and media, it can stand for any development and is of particular relevance to open education.

In order to get a feel for the media interest and stance on MOOCs, here is a sample of headlines from 2012 and 2013:

- The MOOC Revolution: How To Earn An Elite MBA For Free (Schmitt 2013)
- Revolution Hits the Universities (Friedman 2013)
- Will MOOCs Massively Disrupt Higher Education? (Booker 2013)
- How Coursera, a free online education service, will school us all (Kamenetz 2012)
- What MOOCs Will Really Kill Is The Research University (Worstall 2013)
- Embrace Moocs or face decline, warns v-c (Parr 2013)
- MOOCs: End of higher ed as we know it? (Blackenhorn 2012)
- Higher-ed courses with massive enrollments: A revolution starts (Idea 2012)

Writing in early 2014, these headlines already seem dated. Try substituting OER for MOOCs in any of these articles and although the same claims might be made, it becomes apparent that such hyperbolic pieces would not be written about OERs. Often the articles were little more than publicity pieces for the MOOC companies involved, with no critical evaluation of the projected claims. From the open education perspective, the question is why would one branch of open education attract so much excitement, while another one does not?

Education Is Broken

I would contend that the reason MOOCs attracted so much attention – and so little critical evaluation – is because they slotted neatly into a broader set of narratives, in a way that other forms of open education haven't. There are two aspects to this broader narrative: the first is the framing of the problem as 'education is broken', and the second is the overriding Silicon Valley narrative that shapes the form of solutions.

'Education is broken' has become such an accepted standpoint that it is often stated as an irrefutable fact. Andrew D'Souza, the chief operating officer of an educational technology start-up states baldly, 'The education space is massive, very broken' (Tauber 2013); Sebastian Thrun inevitably declared, 'Education is broken. Face it. It is so broken at so many ends, it requires a little bit of Silicon Valley magic' (Wolfson 2013); an influential report from the Institute for Public Policy Research entitled 'An Avalanche is Coming' claimed, 'The models of higher education that marched triumphantly across the globe in the second half of the 20th century are broken' (Barber, Donnelly, & Rizv 2013); even insightful analysts such as Clay Shirky are prone to it, with a piece entitled 'Your Massively Open Offline College Is Broken' (Shirky 2013).

Before considering a response to the broken education claim, there are two questions to ask. The first is, what is meant by a broken system? The second is, why is it stated with such conviction, so often?

To address the first question, we see that what or how education is broken is rarely expanded upon. It is simply stated as a starting position, from which all else follows, a *sine qua non* of educational revolution. Let us assume that this is a genuinely held belief of those who propose it. It is sensible to ask then in what ways might education be broken? At different times it can relate to lack of creativity in K–12 education, or truancy rates, or more often, the financial model of higher education, usually all from a US perspective.

It may well be that there is insufficient creativity in K–12 education, but some of this is a result of scale. Any alternative would need to operate at the scale of a nationwide system and encompass all types of learner. One often sees claims that schooling has remained unchanged for hundreds of years or that it is a system designed for the industrial age; Sal Khan in an interview with *Forbes* claims that education became static over the past 120 years (Khan and Noer 2011). Such claims vastly underestimate the change in pedagogy to more project and group based work that has occurred in schools. As Watters (2012) states, 'To jump from 1892 to 2000 – from the "Committee of Ten" to Khan Academy – ignores the work done by numerous educators and technologists to think about how computers and networks will reshape how we teach and learn.' There are undoubtedly ample opportunities to change how subjects are taught, to engage children and particularly to take advantages of new technology, and one should not underestimate the obstacles in achieving any of this, but it hardly justifies the label of broken.

A point of evidence sometimes claimed for the broken education argument is that truancy is at an all time high (e.g. Paul 2013); therefore, schooling isn't working; therefore, a radical solution is required. However the manner in which truancy rates are recorded varies considerably, and any unauthorised absence, such as a child going on holiday with parents, is now counted as truancy. So before using truancy as evidence that education is fundamentally broken, it is necessary to ask questions such as: Is any change now a statistical one or within the realms of normal variation? Are historical comparisons valid (i.e., are they comparing the same measures)? Can an increase in truancy rates be accounted for by an increase in population or targeted school attendance (e.g. if you are working harder to make sure certain groups are registered in school in the first place, will you get more truancy)? Is it an increase in more pupils being truant, or the same number of truancy pupils being truant for longer? (e.g. one study found that 7% of pupils account for one third of all truancy numbers [Metro 2008]).

This is not to suggest that truancy isn't a serious issue, but it is an example of how making sweeping statements about an entire school system may miss targeting the actual problem groups, which could be more effective. It is also worth noting that truancy or problems at school are often the result of wider societal problems, such as drugs, gun crime, poverty, family breakdown, etc. Isolating school in this mix really does miss the point.

Which brings us to funding, which is the most common candidate for stating that education is broken – that it is financially unsustainable. Spending on education has been increasing, while the return graduates receive in terms of increased salary has been diminishing. In short, higher education is no longer a good return on investment from a purely monetary perspective. Of course, this argument only applies where student fees are paid by the student (such as in the US and UK); other countries, such as Germany, provide free access to higher education. The blame for these rising costs are usually placed at the doors of universities, but in essence they are simply responding to market demands. If students (or their parents) want better facilities such as gyms, cafes and residencies then in order to compete, they have to provide these. In proposing MOOCs as the solution to these funding problems, most commentators fail to appreciate the demands that would be placed on MOOCs if they moved from a secondary, supplementary position in education to a central, primary one.

For instance, when Shirky (2012) promotes MOOCs as the equivalent of MP3 or YouTube, he underestimates the demands that will be put on them, and is uncharacteristically wrong about the analogy. MP3s could replace vinyl/CDs completely. Free MOOCs can't replace the higher education system because much of the cost of education has little to do with the educating element. Taking a MOOC for interest is one thing, but when career prospects depend on it, then different demands will be placed on MOOCs that currently don't exist. If MOOCs were to replace higher education, they would need to find ways of realising the following:

- Dealing with student appeals
- Coping with a diverse range of students and abilities
- Ensuring quality control of content
- Developing assessment methods and procedures that can be defended
- Ensuring robustness of service
- Ensuring accreditation reliability and trustworthiness
- Complying with numerous regulations on issues such as accessibility
- Ensuring a supply of high-quality course production
- Providing pastoral care

All of these requirements have financial implications beyond the current content focus (which is subsidised by the very universities that MOOCs are supposed to replace). Inevitably, MOOCs as universal education method would soon begin to cost more and more. They may be cheaper than the existing model, which would be dramatic, but they would soon cease to be free or open.

It is not the focus of this book to explore various funding models for higher education, but the 'education is broken' argument is rarely stated as 'funding for education is broken', and if the debate that society needs to have is about how to fund higher education, then that should be the focus rather than a proxy argument around broken education and alternative models.

The argument is too simplistic and just lazy; as with the truancy case, there are a number of factors that would need exploring for an effective solution. But there is also a more manipulative intention to it, which relates to the language of change and how it shapes our responses. If something is diagnosed as broken, then the appropriate response is to fix it. The search then becomes for a solution, and very often those people who are determining education to be broken also stand to profit from providing an alternative solution. For instance, the authors of the 'Avalanche' report in the UK all work for the education publisher and courseware provider Pearson. Both D'Souza and Thrun, quoted above, were CEOs of companies that seek to offer a solution to the problem of broken education. There is even an education start-up (degreed.com) that ran a campaign with the slogan 'Education is broken. Someone should do something.' That someone being them, naturally.

Caulfield (2012) highlights the difference between a rhetoric of opportunity and a rhetoric of crisis. This difference in language is significant for framing our response. Thibodeau and Boroditsky found that the metaphors used to frame a problem influenced the solution that subjects proposed, so whether crime was couched in terms of a virus- or a beast-like metaphor, would shape how people thought it should be handled. A rhetoric of opportunity might suggest encouraging those already working in the sector to take advantage of opportunities and work with others. A rhetoric of crisis suggests that the incumbents cannot be trusted and that external agents are required to make sweeping changes.

Education is broken; it therefore requires fixing, and MOOCs provide the radical solution required. This was the simplistic logic that underpinned many of the early MOOC articles. It is easy to see how MOOCs can be posited as a solution to the nebulous problem of broken education – they are free, online, and infinitely scalable. The same could be said of OERs also, so why do MOOCs appeal to this rhetoric of crisis in a way that other open education movements have not? The reasons relate to the second dominant narrative that they have sympathy with, namely that of Silicon Valley.

The Silicon Valley Narrative

The model of Silicon Valley provides such a powerful narrative that it has come to dominate thinking far beyond that of computing. For instance, Staton (2014) declares that the degree is doomed because Silicon Valley avoids hiring people with computer science degrees and prefers those with good community presence on software developer sites. From this he concludes this model is applicable across all domains and vocations. It hardly needs adding that Staton is the CEO of an educational company.

There are several elements necessary to the Silicon Valley narrative: firstly, that a technological fix is both possible and in existence; secondly, that external forces will change, or disrupt, an existing sector; thirdly, that wholesale revolution is required; lastly, that the solution is provided by commerce.

We have seen how the 'education is broken' meme satisfies the third condition of the Silicon Valley narrative. If it is accepted as broken, then only a revolution is sufficient to resolve it. MOOCs appeal to the first and second of these conditions. They are a very technologically driven solution, particularly in their xMOOC instantiation. Thrun famously worked at Google, where he developed the driverless car. The artificial intelligence promise of adaptive learning systems and sophisticated automatic assessment is appealing in that it seems futuristic, and it aligns with the Silicon Valley technological solution approach.

Although Thrun, Koller and Ng all worked at Stanford, and so could thus be seen as part of the establishment, Thrun in particular has been cast as the education outsider. In order to satisfy this need for an external party coming to the aid of the sector, the Khan Academy's founder, Sal Khan, has often been proposed as the godfather of MOOCs (High 2013).

Another important aspect that appeals to Silicon Valley, entrepreneurs and journalists alike is that of disruption. This comes from Clayton Christensen's influential 1997 work, *The Innovator's Dilemma*, which analysed how digital technology in particular could create new markets which disrupted existing ones. Christensen made the distinction between sustaining technologies, which help improve an existing market, and disruptive ones, which establish a new market. Digital cameras can be seen as disruptive to the traditional camera market, while improved memory and features of digital cameras are sustaining.

It is a term that has been applied much more broadly than its original concept, to the point where it is almost meaningless and rarely critically evaluated. Dvorak (2004) complains that it is essentially meaningless, stating that 'There is no such thing as a disruptive technology. There are inventions and new ideas, many of which fail while others succeed. That's it.' There remains however a disruption obsession inherent in the Silicon Valley narrative. As Watters (2013) argues, disruption has become somewhat akin to a cultural myth amongst Silicon Valley:

> When I say then, that 'disruptive innovation' is one of the great myths of the contemporary business world, particularly of the tech industry, I don't mean by 'myth' that Clayton Christensen's explanation of changes to

markets and business models and technologies is a false-hood... my assigning 'myth' to 'disruptive innovation' is meant to highlight the ways in which this narrative has been widely accepted as unassailably true.

Nobody wants to just create a useful tool; it has to disrupt an industry. Education, perceived as slow, resistant to change and old-fashioned, is seen as ripe for disruption. Christensen, Horn and Johnson (2008) themselves have deemed it so, stating, 'disruption is a necessary and overdue chapter in our public schools.' Hence the Avalanche report justifies itself by claiming that all of the key 'elements of the traditional university are threatened by the coming avalanche. In Clayton Christensen's terms, universities are ripe for disruption.' In his criticism of the impact of OERs, Kortemeyer (2013) states, 'OERs have not noticeably disrupted the traditional business model of higher education,' because for something to be successful, only disruption counts.

We can see many of these elements in essays on MOOCs. Let us take Clay Shirky's essay 'Your Massively Open Offline College Is Broken' (2013), as it generated a lot of interest and was considered to be a thoughtful analysis. In terms of our narrative essentials, Shirky even has the 'education is broken' meme in the title of his piece, and later states it boldly: 'I have a different answer: School is broken and everyone knows it.' He sets out a reasonably convincing case about the finance issues associated with higher education, although he does not question finance models. Shirky cites a book *Don't go back to school* (Stark 2013) which interviewed 100 people who had dropped out of school and gone on to be successful. Largely they then self-teach themselves using internet resources, an example of the Silicon Valley model being applied broadly.

In his previous essay, 'Napster, Udacity and the Academy' (Shirky 2012), he compares the impact of MOOCs on higher education with that of the MP3 on the music industry. This conforms to the Silicon Valley narrative, proposing a revolution and disruption: 'Higher education is now being disrupted; our MP3 is the massive open online course (or MOOC).' It also suggests that the commercial, external provider will be the force of change, stating, 'Our Napster is Udacity, the education startup.'

All of the elements can also be seen in Clark's (2013) piece where he declares that (referring to Khan) 'It took a hedge fund manager to shake up education because he didn't have any HE baggage.' It appeals to the Silicon Valley narrative to have a saviour riding in from outside HE to save it. If the influence of those inside higher education, such as Wiley, Downes, Siemens, etc., is acknowledged, that weakens the appeal of the story.

Kernohan (2013) performed a semantic analysis of eleven popular MOOC articles. Taking Kernohan's articles to conduct simple word counts the word 'disrupt' (or derivative) occurred 12 times, 'revolution' 16, and 'company' 17. Obviously this is a selective choice of terms ('open' appears 48 times for comparison), but the presence of these terms indicates a particular framing of the MOOC story that allies with the Silicon Valley narrative.

We can now see why MOOCs proved so popular with journalists. Firstly they seem to offer a solution to the 'education is broken' meme, which had been gaining currency. Secondly, they met all the criteria for the Silicon Valley narrative: they proposed a technological solution, they could be framed as the result of external forces and they provided a revolutionary model. Nearly all the early MOOC articles framed them as disruptive to the standard higher education model. And they were established as separate companies outside of higher education, thus providing interest around business models and potential profits by disrupting the sector. This heady mix proved too irresistible for many technology or education journalists.

This analysis also reveals why other open education initiatives haven't garnered as much attention. They often seek to supplement or complement education, thus ruining the 'education is broken' argument. Similarly, they are often conducted by those who work in higher education, which undermines the narrative of external agents promoting change on a sector that is out of touch. And lastly, they are supported by not-for-profit institutions, which does not fit the model of new, disruptive businesses emerging. If one wanted to make an argument for disruption, then open textbooks could make a convincing case, since they undermine an established business with digital, low-cost alternatives, but as projects like OpenStax are not-for-profit, they do not fit the Silicon Valley narrative as neatly as MOOCs.

One further aspect of the Silicon Valley and disruption narrative is that it demands a 'year zero' mentality. It is a much more convincing story if someone can be said to have invented a new way of working. Because complete genesis invention is rare, most work is tinkering with old ideas and improving them, this often requires either a wilful ignorance of past work or an imaginative reworking of it.

Back to the Future, Again

2013 saw a number of MOOC-related discoveries and breakthroughs, which bore at least a passing resemblance to established educational practice. For example, we saw the BBC (Coughlan 2013) announcing Harvard's innovative trialling of the 'SPOC – a small, private online course' that would take the advantages of MOOCs, but place them in a safer, enclosed environment for fee-paying campus students. It took quite some imagining to see how this varied from the online courses that most universities had been running for the past decade, but rebranding it under the MOOC umbrella rendered it new. As we have already seen, Coursera similarly decided that campus based elearning might be an effective market for MOOCs, when they partnered with ten universities. As well as SPOCs we had Micro-MOOCs, which were 'short e-courses', DOCCs (Distributed Open Collaborative Course) and SOOCs (Social Online Open Course or Small Open Online Course).

Clayton Christensen seemed to come to the conclusion that totally online learning in K–12 was not going to arrive soon or that it might not be desirable, and a blended learning approach, which many schools had practiced for years, could be beneficial. Rather than view this as a sustaining technology or a failure of disruption, it was labelled 'hybrid pedagogy' and touted as 'a fundamentally new concept [in] the world of disruptive innovation' (Christensen, Horn and Staker 2013).

EdX declared that it was hard and expensive to create quality online courses, (Kolowich 2013d) and Sebastian Thrun attributed his Udacity pivot to the finding that retaining open entry learners is difficult (Chafkin 2013). In the Khan interview mentioned above, most pedagogic theories developed over the past 120 years are ignored and then attributed to Khan.

Henry Petroski (2012) suggests that society forgets fundamental lessons in bridge design every 30 years, because that is the average length of an engineering career. The same may be true with educational technology, except that it is a form of wilful amnesia. Educators have been designing large-scale distance courses, and then large-scale online courses, for over 40 years, and yet much of the MOOC movement has chosen to ignore this experience.

Some of the rebranding around MOOCs is an inevitable and beneficial side effect of the increased interest in elearning that they generated. Labelling an online course a SPOC may seem strange, but it is not harmful. There is, however, a more devious element in some of the amnesia, which relates to the Silicon Valley narrative. It inflates the value of the innovation if it can lay claim to inventing a wholly new approach, and it also undermines the status of incumbents in an industry if their contribution is dismissed or forgotten, rendering the role of external agents more viable.

This is not to suggest some higher-level conspiracy generating from Silicon Valley, but the essential ingredients of the Silicon Valley narrative constitute what might be viewed as a conspiracy of sentiment. It appeals to a worldview that entrepreneurs, investors, journalists and technologists implicitly hold and reinforce. As Watters puts it, 'The version of history they offer is quite telling, as it reflects how they perceive the past, how they want the rest of us to perceive the past, as well as how they hope we'll move into the future.'

Conclusions

All of this might not matter; most disciplines will complain that their coverage in the general media is overly simplistic or biased – one has only to think of the coverage of health issues, for instance. Indeed, it could be seen as a blessing. Any media coverage helps to make future funding more likely and makes internal projects more viable. Having been involved in the early forms of MOOCs, I know from personal experience that there has been a change in receptiveness from research funders to conducting research into open courses since the MOOC bubble began.

Nor is this simply a matter of historical pedantry, a desire to ensure that early MOOC pioneers are assured their rightful place in history. While historical accuracy is always desirable, it does not impact how people use the legacy of that discovery once a victor has been determined. However, there is more at stake than simple journalistic accuracy. In Chapter 1, I argued that there is a battle for narrative in open education, and that narrative will have a strong influence on the future direction it takes. If MOOCs are the most prominent aspect of open education, then the narrative associated with them will create an impact for other aspects. If the dominant narrative is that of Silicon Valley, then this frames what is deemed the appropriate model for other forms of open education. If you wish to create an open course, then the model for doing so and criteria for deciding what it should achieve has been determined to serve the needs of this overriding weltenschauung. Or if you wanted to structure a programme for releasing low-cost staff outputs (the sort of thing we will examine in the next chapter), you could find yourself being asked to couch it in terms of MOOCs.

All of this is not to suggest that the MOOC phenomena hasn't been important both in terms of the education sector itself and more significantly, for learners. As Siemens (2012) stated, 'Anyone who goes out and educates, or at least provides a learning opportunity for people in developing parts of the world and does so without cost and increases their prospect for opportunities, in my eyes is a terrific idea.' It might seem churlish to complain about the tone of press coverage when set against the thousands of learners who have had positive, even life-changing experiences in MOOCs. The aim of this chapter was not to provide a critique of MOOCs and their applications (which was covered in the preceding chapter), but rather to use MOOC coverage to examine the manner in which open education is influenced by competing narratives.

Similarly, the aim of this chapter is not to suggest that Silicon Valley commercial solutions are not useful or innovative. One has only to look at the impact Google has had on society in general – and education in particular – to see how successful this can be. Universities have their own demands and methods of functioning, and often it is necessary to operate outside of these to create a specific product for popular uptake. The intention in this chapter was rather to draw attention to the importance of narrative and how it shapes perception and direction. MOOCs in particular have seen the openness narrative overtaken by other, more dominant ones. It may be that you conclude this is necessary or inevitable to gain the impact MOOCs have had, but we should at least be aware of the influence of this narrative and whether alternative ones are possible.

One of the negative implications of the 'education is broken' / Silicon Valley narrative is that it necessarily frames all change as revolution. This creates a false dichotomy amongst the audience, who either accept the revolution and all that it encompasses or are seen as opposing it and wishing to preserve the status quo. To be suspicious of the motives of those who declare education to be broken or to question the nature of this claim is not the same as proclaiming that there are no problems in education. Similarly, being dismissive of the concept of disruption is not equivalent to being resistant to change.

Another downside to the revolution-based narrative is that it requires excessive claims to be made in order to justify the scale of the revolution, such as Thrun's declaration that there will be only 10 providers of global education, or that MOOCS will mean the end of the university and provide free global education for all. Inevitably, these predictions are failing – Thrun has changed direction with Udacity, EdX found that linking employers with MOOC learners was not successful and that 'existing HR departments want to go for traditional degree programs and filter out nontraditional candidates' (Kolowich 2013d) and a school designed to provide community while students studied MOOCs of their choice has struggled to retain students (Caplan-Bricker 2013). The MOOC backlash has begun, with some university staff refusing to use MOOC material or participate in MOOCs (Kolowich 2013e) and much online comment now taking on a critical tone, for example, Laurillard's (2014) 'Five Myths About MOOCs'. It is debatable whether these reactions would have been seen if MOOCs had not been oversold, and there is a danger that the backlash will undermine future MOOC development.

Openness in education offers many real opportunities to improve education in terms of the opportunities for learners, developing pedagogies based on open practice, distributing free resources and democratising education. Many of these radical changes are being driven by those who work in education, but the Silicon Valley narrative wishes to exclude this part of the story. MOOCs have highlighted how the battle for narrative shapes the direction that an innovation can take. It may be MOOCs currently, but the same pattern is likely to occur with whatever the next open education innovation might be, because there is a powerful story to be told around global education, and the size of the education market is irresistible to the Silicon Valley narrative. Recognising this struggle for narrative and constructing alternatives is therefore at the heart of the battle for open. One method of doing so is to utilise the power of the internet for academics to share their practice openly. This is the subject of the next chapter.

CHAPTER 7

Open Scholarship

The guerrilla band should not be considered inferior against the army which it fights simply because it has inferior firepower.

—Che Guevara

Introduction

In the previous three chapters the focus has largely been on projects and institutional practices. These large-scale movements are shaping the open education landscape and are where the key features of the battle for open are most evidently manifest. However, just as significant are the individual practices that shape the paths and features within that landscape. This chapter will look at how individual academics are adapting their own scholarly practices by adopting open approaches.

My previous book was entitled 'The Digital Scholar' (Weller 2011), but it could have just as aptly been called 'The Open Scholar'. 'Digital' and 'open' are not necessarily synonymous of course – someone could create all their outputs in digital format but store them on a local hard disk, publish in journals that are not open access and not establish an online identity. This could be termed digital scholarship, but the digital element here does not indicate any substantial alteration in practice. In my previous book I suggested that 'digital scholar' was really a shorthand for the intersection of three elements: digital, networked and open. The first two are necessary conditions, but it is really the open aspect that brings about change in scholarly practice that is worth commenting on.

Open practice has an obvious relationship with higher education. As Wiley and Green (2012) put it, 'Education is, first and foremost, an enterprise of sharing. In fact, sharing is the sole means by which education is effected.' Apart from rare (and they are much rarer than many academics believe) cases of commercial advantage regarding research, sharing as widely as possible should be at the heart of educational practice. The digital, network, open triad makes this sharing easier, drastically alters the scale at which it can be achieved and removes obstacles and costs associated with doing so, but it arises from this fundamental point that sharing is central to education.

Veletsianos and Kimmons (2012) propose that open scholarship takes three forms:

> (1) open access and open publishing, (2) open education, including open educational resources and open teaching, and (3) networked participation, concluding that open scholarship is a set of phenomena and practices surrounding scholars' uses of digital and networked technologies underpinned by certain grounding assumptions regarding openness and democratization of knowledge creation and dissemination.

Most of these practices, such as open access publishing and open teaching, have been covered elsewhere in this book, so this chapter will focus on three elements: what Veletsianos and Kimmons call 'networked participation', which is individual activity across various media and networks; online identity and how it relates to traditional academic practice; and new possibilities in research practice that open techniques give rise to.

As with previous chapters, the aim is not to provide the definitive overview of open scholarship as a topic, but to focus on how openness is significant as part of mainstream practice. This subject is less well defined than that of MOOCs, OERs and Open Access, as it addresses changes to academic behaviour afforded by open practice and technology. These three areas (networked practice, identity and new research approaches) then can be seen as representing a particular take on open scholarship, which in reality subsumes the previous chapters also.

Networked Practice

When I wrote *The Digital Scholar* in 2010/2011, the picture regarding academic use of social media and new technologies was one of wariness. Proctor, Williams and Stewart (2010) summed it up, saying, 'Frequent or intensive use is rare, and some researchers regard blogs, wikis and other novel forms of communication as a waste of time or even dangerous.' This 'approach with caution' attitude still seems to prevail, with Esposito (2013) reporting 'a cautious interest in Web 2.0 tools to support inquiry activities'. Similarly Gruzd, Staves and Wilk (2012) report that most research institutions do not make use of online profiles when considering promotion, but they suggest this is beginning to change.

What has changed is the increased adoption of social media tools amongst society in general, so academics are more likely to have an identity in such places that mixes professional and personal. There has also been an increase in academic-specific sites such as Academia.edu, ResearchGate and Mendeley. Academia.edu (2013) reported nearly 9 million registered users in 2013, and ResearchGate over 3 million, although how many of these are active is not clear. The combination of these two factors means that academics are more likely to have some form of online identity.

Veletsianos (2012) identifies seven ways in which scholars use Twitter: to share information, resources and media; to share information about teaching; to request assistance from and respond to requests from others; to engage in social commentary; to engage in digital identity and impression management; to explicitly network and connect with others; and to highlight their participation in other networks, for example, linking to blogs. This corresponds with work by Fransman et al. (2011) at the OU who found that 26% of academics had Twitter accounts, which while not a majority, represents a significant uptake from the very specialised adoption of such tools previously. These were used in a variety of ways, such as communicating within project teams, disseminating findings and musing and generating research questions.

The higher-education focused sites such as Academia.edu represent a 'safe' or more obviously relevant route to establishing an online identity for many academics. These sites relate explicitly to academic practice, compared with general social media, which many academics perceive as frivolous or irrelevant. As one respondent in the Fransman study stated, 'The problem is I'm not really sure what the function of Twitter or these other technologies are or at least how I would use them.' And others view them with suspicion and fear; one participant claimed, 'You wouldn't send your history article round to the world and his wife because you'd end up with it not being yours! And even once you've published it you have to be careful because of the copyright so you can't just stick it anywhere.'

In declaring the rise of open scholarship then, one must be careful not to overstate the case. As with many other aspects of open education, the story of open scholarship has been one of steady adaptation and growth rather than sudden revolution. Selwyn (2010) cautions that there is a strong tendency of solipsism from educational technologists relating to social media and openness. Discussions about the potential of social media in education are 'self-contained, self-referencing and self-defining ... These are generally conversations that only ever take place between groups of social media–using educators – usually using social media to talk about the educational benefits of social media.'

This does however create a dilemma for educators, since the direction of social media and openness will be influenced by their actions. As we saw with OERs, it is necessary to go through a belief-driven stage in order to construct the context wherein impact can be measured. Empirical observation of what has happened forms a fundamental approach for the objective researcher when examining the effects on society at large, but in terms of shaping their own domain, it is an excessively passive approach that would be self-fulfilling or defeating, depending on one's perspective. It also presents the current context as neutral, which may not be the case. The presence of many institutional practices may actively discourage open scholarship. For example, the relationship to tenure and the advice that Cheverie et al. (2009) found was that 'word of mouth to younger colleagues discourages digital scholarship in the hiring, tenure and promotion process.' Open scholarship is unique amongst interests for academics because it is an as yet undefined area that is both about scholarship and defined by them. This indicates that there is a tension between the context in which academics operate and the potential of open scholarship, which relates to academic identity.

The Open Scholar and Identity

Open scholarship creates new opportunities and tensions for individuals, and one means of examining these is to consider the concept of academic identity. In this section, general theories of identity will briefly be considered, academic identity in particular. We will then consider how open scholarship impacts on these notions of identity and the relationship with traditional forms of academic identity.

The pioneering work on identity is that of Mead (1934), who argued that one's concept of self is most fully developed when community attitudes and values are integrated. A strong component in the construction of identity is the degree to which either we absorb the values of the community we are in or find a community whose values we can absorb comfortably, summarised in the dictum 'self reflects society'. The strength of these identities has tangible behaviours – the salience of religious identity correlates with time spent on religious activities (Stryker and Serpe 1982), for example. This social view is echoed by Snow (2001), who stated that identity is largely socially constructed and, as well as belonging, includes a sense of difference from other communities. In this framing, identity is seen as 'a shared sense of "one-ness" or "we-ness" anchored in shared attributes and experiences & in contrast to one or more sets of "others"'. Looking at national identity, Canetti (1962) determined that 'crowd symbols' are significant in constructing these shared values. He argued that for England, the sea is a crowd symbol, while for the French it was the Revolution. These crowd symbols, he contested, were more significant than history or territory and represented common, well-understood symbols, which could sustain a popular feeling of nationhood.

With regards to academic identity, Henkel (2005) identifies a number of significant attributes, with autonomy important amongst these, highlighting that 'autonomy is integrally related to academic identity.' Changes in the structure of higher education has meant that the department an individual belongs to is now not as central to their identity as it once was. Henkel argues, 'The department is now only one, and not necessarily the most secure or important, focus of academic activity and identification.' Becher (1989) stresses the importance of disciplines in academic identity, arguing that academia can be seen as comprising distinctive 'tribes', with their territory established through rules and conventions as significant as the knowledge domain itself.

Turning to aspects of open scholarship, blogs probably represent the most established form. Ewins (2005) uses the postmodern term 'multiphrenic' to describe the multiple identities that authors project, with perhaps a different one for their discipline, their campus based persona and their online persona. It is false to think of any of these as a 'true' identity; they project different aspects of the individual, which are related to the social norms of that context. Dennen (2009) points out that at the genesis of a blog, the academic must make decisions about that identity: What type of tone will the blog adopt? What topics will it cover? How much of the author's personal life should be revealed? She suggests that, just as on campus there exists a set of social norms, so it is online, and the blogger responds to these. These identity norms spread across the highly connected blogosphere 'based on a viral movement of individual actions across blogs.'

These new identities can be in conflict with traditional ones, as Costa (2013) argues, stating, 'Higher education institutions are more likely to encourage conventional forms of publication than innovative approaches to research communication.' She goes on to suggest that although universities are not opposed to change, their own identity is deeply associated with certain traditions, which are reinforced through 'strategies that coerce individuals to play by the rules' and the creation of certain myths.

Bringing these strands together, we can establish a picture of the open scholar and how their identity relates to practice. The notion of crowd symbols from national identity has an equivalence with central tenets of disciplinary belief, be these iconic papers or methods. As a member of an academic discipline these crowd symbols help define identity. However, as Dennen points out, blogging, and by extension other forms of online identity, have their own social norms, which could be seen as a set of competing crowd symbols. The online identity may also provide a route to re-establishing core academic values such as autonomy.

Open scholars are thus in a rather schizophrenic position. They can occupy two different domains, which may have competing values. For example, the open scholarship community places a precedent on immediacy, sharing small outputs and working through ideas in the open. The traditional disciplinary community places more value on considered, larger outputs and not releasing these until late in the research process. For open scholars the intersection of these sometimes competing social norms can create tension.

By way of analogy, we can think of open scholars as any group in a nation that has a strong local identity which may be at odds with their national one. This can be seen with mountain dwellers, who have a strong affinity with other mountain folk, as well as with their own nation. Analysing those who live in the Swiss Alps, Debarbieux and Rudaz (2008) found that 'mountain people throughout the world – beyond their cultural, religious or political differences – easily feel at one' and that 'A mountain farmer in the Valais canton has more in common with a mountain farmer in Nepal than with someone living on the Swiss Plateau.' For those who live in the Alps, they have a dual identity which crosses the various borders, so there is a strong Alpine community which transcends national borders, but at other times, their national identity will have prevalence. For instance, when dealing with weather they are predominantly Alpine, but when it comes to supporting a football team they may revert to their national identity and be French, Italian, Swiss, etc. Many of us have this multiple identity, but it is less complicated for those who dwell in cities. Whilst someone might classify themselves as a Londoner and British, the urban identity operates at a distinct level to the national one, whereas, for Alpine people these identities can intersect and overlap.

Open scholars find themselves in a similar position, having a loyalty to their discipline, but also working within social norms in the open community. By considering the norms of the two communities it is possible to identify tensions and determine the benefits of each in realizing scholarly functions. With regards to the battle for open, academic identity can be seen as an influencing factor in all of the broader movements. For example, open access publishing relates to how a researcher shares their work, and a publication record can be seen as a core element in academic identity for many. Similarly, the use and sharing of teaching content through OERs and MOOCs is fundamental to the identity of educators. Understanding how openness relates to identity and how it is being shaped by online practice may seem like an interesting but peripheral concept, but it will determine the shape of open education. In the next section, this will be explored in more detail by examining how open scholarship can affect one particular practice.

The Art of Guerilla Research

We are accustomed in academia to conceptualising research as having certain components: it is often externally funded research, and it produces a traditional output such as a journal article or book. We think of research as having a certain 'size' for something to count. One of the implications of open scholarship, though, is that it creates different ways of approaching research. The dominant attitude towards how research is conducted was shaped prior to the arrival of digital, networked and open technologies. Some of that attitude is undoubtedly still valid, but there are also a host of possibilities that are prohibited by remaining wedded solely to that view.

One such aspect is what might be termed a Do It Yourself and Do It Now approach. For instance, establishing a journal was an arduous task that needed negotiations with publishers and a sufficient business model to be workable. For some areas, such as interdisciplinary journals, the projected market might be too small to be economically worthwhile. However, the development of open online journal software such as OJS and Google's Annotum removes many of these considerations. An individual could start a journal in an afternoon. I experimented with creating a Meta EdTech journal (Weller 2011), which republished open access journal articles I selected from other journals (as an experiment into the possibilities rather than as a serious journal). Such a journal could feature original contributions, be experimental in format or create an interdisciplinary journal by republishing existing articles with a commentary. No permission is required to create it, and it can operate at low cost. Of course, one might argue that the presence of a publisher provides legitimacy, but if the individual (or team) have sufficient networked identities, then that creates its own form of legitimacy.

Another form of research might be to create an app; for instance, when a team at the OU created Facebook apps for students (Weller 2007), their working assumption was that they would act as if they were external parties and not have access to any privileged information. Although it required specialist software development in the spare time of one of the team, the apps were developed for no cost and with no permission required. Building apps might be a legitimate means to gather research data.

A third example is the interrogation of open data. Tony Hirst's blog gives many examples of mining data from government sites or social media tools such as Twitter to investigate hypotheses. He investigated how influential spending data was on local council decisions (Hirst 2013), or who was tweeting links relating to a BBC television programme and how they were connected (Hirst 2012). Another approach is to use public writing as a textual source; for instance, travel blogs have proved to be a rich seam of research data, producing articles on identity (Kane 2012), marketing (Schmallegger and Carson 2008) and methodology (Banyai and Glover 2012).

I should stress that none of these examples are meant to supplant traditional approaches to research. They are not superior to them, but in addition to them. They are often complementary also. An initial piece of individual low-cost research may form the basis for bidding for funding for more substantial work.

What is common to all of these, and indeed to many of the open education approaches such as the original MOOCs, is that they do not require permission, except maybe some relating to time allocation. In his review of the film *The Social Network,* Creative Commons founder Larry Lessig (2010) pointed out that it was this removal of permission barriers that was the really significant part of the Facebook story: 'What's important here is that

Zuckerberg's genius could be embraced by half a billion people within six years of its first being launched, without (and here is the critical bit) asking permission of anyone. The real story is not the invention. It is the platform that makes the invention sing.'

This same freedom applies to scholarly practice also, including how we conduct research, disseminate results, and teach. This 'just do it' approach can adopt a term from software development: 'guerrilla research'. Unger and Warfel (2011) argue persuasively for it, claiming that 'Guerrilla research methods are faster, lower-cost methods that provide sufficient enough insights to make informed strategic decisions.'

Guerrilla research has the following characteristics:

- It can be done by one or two researchers and does not require a team.
- It relies on existing open data, information and tools.
- It is fairly quick to realise.
- It is often disseminated via blogs and social media.
- It doesn't require permission.

As stated, guerrilla research needn't be in competition with formal, funded research. In fact it's a good way to get started on this. If a researcher needs to demonstrate to a funder that a project is worth investing in, then being able to show some interesting preliminary findings is useful, as is the ability to demonstrate through illustrative analytics that the blogs and tweets of their initial findings generated a certain level of interest.

Some of the inherent waste in current practice often goes unnoticed, because it is accepted practice that academics have been enculturated into. For example, some researchers can spend considerable time, months even, developing research bids to submit to funders. Stevenson (2013) calculated 3 months for a proposal, but the Research Councils UK found that 12 days for a conventional proposal was the average (RCUK 2006). The success rates of bids are decreasing as it becomes more competitive; for instance, the ESRC state that only 17% of bids were successful in 2009–10 (ESRC 2010). If a bid is unsuccessful then sometimes it will be modified and submitted elsewhere, but often it is simply abandoned and the researcher moves on to the next one. That equates to a lot of lost time and knowledge. The RCUK report in 2006 estimated that £196 million was spent on applications to the eight UK research councils, most of which was staff time. The number of applications increases every year – there were 2,800 bids submitted to ESRC in 2009–10, an increase in 33% from 2005–6, so this figure is likely to have increased significantly. Some of these 2,800 proposals were studentships, which have a higher success rate, but even taking an optimistic figure of 800 bids accepted to account for studentships, this still leaves 2,000 failed bids. If we take RCUK's figure of 12 days as an average per bid, then this equates to 65 years of effort, and this is just one of several major research councils in the UK and Europe to whom researchers will be bidding. Obviously this is just an indicative figure, and there are many assumptions in its calculation that one could challenge, but nevertheless, the nature of research as it is currently conceived has a lot of waste assumed within it. This is not to suggest that the peer-review process is not valid, but that the failure to capitalise on rejected bids represents a substantial waste of resources. As with open source software and OER approaches to teaching, open approaches to research may provide a more efficient method.

Many of these bids represent valid research and may fail on technicalities relating to the proposal format. Guerrilla research may represent a means of realising some of these, although in some areas, particularly science, it isn't possible. However, a more open approach to research development would reduce the overall wastage. The competitive nature of bidding often precludes public sharing of bids, though, especially in the development stage, and as such, it represents one of those areas of tension between open scholarship and traditional practice.

Conclusions

Open scholarship could be a book in itself, and there are many aspects of it here that have not been covered. Citizen science is one such area, where academics are developing platforms and approaches to engage the wider public in science have seen great success. For example, projects such as iSpot allow users to take photographs of different species and ask for identification, and this can be used to plot the distribution of certain species. Open data, changes to the peer review system to make it post review, establishing online communities – all of these are fruitful areas of open scholarship. The focus here has been to demonstrate one particular aspect, that of research, and how it can be affected by open practice, but the same can be applied to teaching or public engagement or any other form of scholarly activity.

Open scholarship is not without its issues. Although privacy is distinct – since open scholarship is about choosing to share certain aspects and privacy is about the unpermitted invasion of those elements that one chooses not to make public – many feel uncomfortable with any form of online presence. It may be that having such an identity is now an integral part of being a scholar, so an element of compulsion underlies some of the proselytising about open scholarship. This is particularly true of learners, some of whom may have legitimate reasons for not wishing to establish an identity in the open (for example, if they have been the victims of cyberstalking). Learning is inherently an uncomfortable process, a learner is moving from a position of (relative) ignorance to one of (relative) expertise. Implicit in this process is exposing some of that ignorance. As even one of the advocates of open teaching, George Siemens (2014), stresses we should not forget the vulnerability of learning. Thus a closed, safe environment such as an institutional learning platform may provide the right context for many learners.

It is, however, also part of the role of education to equip learners with the skills as well as the knowledge they need. Increasingly this will involve the development of digital or web literacies. These are not the subject of this book, but operating effectively and safely in the open and constructing an appropriate online identity will be key amongst them. For example, Jim Groom has founded the Domain of One's Own project out of University of Maryland Washington (Udell 2012). This provides all students with their own domain names and web space. As well as maintaining their own blog on WordPress, they can install other software and 'carve out their own space on the web that they own and control'. They can take over ownership of this when they graduate. Groom sees this level of control, linked to the individual not the institution, essential in establishing an online identity.

It is also necessary to be wary about the downside of operating in the open; there are numerous stories of people being dismissed from jobs for injudicious posting or tweeting, and academics should not feel immune from this. Perhaps of greater concern is the manner in which others may wilfully misuse open debate against the academic. Many educational bloggers take up blogging precisely because it allows them to comment on political issues and the state of higher education. The UK blogger who uses the pseudonym Plashing Vole frequently criticises the UK government and found himself threatened by a national newspaper with a potential story calling for his resignation (Plashing Vole 2013). The story did not run in the end, but even the existence of the threat is enough to make some scholars worry about operating in the open.

The battle for open in terms of open scholarship is less well defined than in other aspects of open education, perhaps because it is a less well defined area itself. It is less a battle with external forces usurping practice, but more an internal one, between existing practice and the opportunities available. The relationship with commerce is one that is less fraught here; academics will use commercial sites such as Twitter, ResearchGate, Slideshare, etc., for as long as they are useful. The functions these support are part of a richer mix of the open scholar's identity, so any one is less vital than the fundamentals of publishing or teaching, where the commercial interests have created greater tension.

The discussion of the identity of open scholars reveals that there is a tension within education itself, which is of more significance. As universities increase their awareness of the value of open scholarship to their own reputational brand, so more of them create guidelines for how to operate. Generally these are helpful and aimed at supporting the open scholar, but as more of the world moves online, so the potential damage from the types of 'Twitter storms' we see elsewhere increases. This creates a possible tension for the open scholar and the institution. The reason many scholars operate in the open is the freedom it offers; this liberty is perhaps the key characteristic of open scholarship, as we saw with the potential for guerrilla research. As with early MOOCs, open access publishing and use of OERs, what open scholarship permits is experimentation and autonomy, and that may be the direction the battle takes in this area.

We have now looked at the four main areas of open education that this book covers, open access, open education resources, MOOCs and open scholarship. In each of these a case can be made for the success of the open approach and its shift into the mainstream of educational practice. Simultaneously, in each area there are issues that arise that are specifically related to the new challenges of openness. The central argument of this book, that openness has been successful but now faces a battle for its future direction, is manifest in each of these four topics, but the exact nature of the success and the tensions varies with each. Having demonstrated the nature of the battle for open in these four specific areas, the last three chapters will return to considering the overall argument.

CHAPTER 8

Openness Uncovered

Everything is post these days, as if we're all just a footnote
to something earlier that was real enough to have a name of
its own.

—Margaret Atwood

Introduction

While setting out the manner in which openness has been successful, this book has thus far presented it as a largely beneficial approach. While it does have many benefits, there are also problems and issues associated with an open approach. One of the consequences of many of the open education developments being conducted in an adversarial manner, with commercial interests such as publishers either resisting it or others attempting to claim it, is that advocates of open education often feel they are forced to ignore any potential issues, lest they are seized upon to discredit the whole approach. This may be analogous to climate change scientists who have been reluctant to voice concerns about specific pieces of data or interpretations, because any doubts will be used to undermine the overall message.

This is yet another consequence of there being a battle for openness. As with the disruption myth we saw in Chapter 6, it forces people into extremes. Therefore, in this chapter, some of the criticisms and issues surrounding openness will be explored. Even after arguing for an open, intellectual commons, James Boyle (2008) stresses that, 'It is not that openness is always right. It is not. … Rather, it is that we need a balance between open and closed, owned and free, and we are systematically likely to get the balance wrong.' Similarly, Dave Cormier (2009), who coined the term MOOC and is a proponent of open practice, warns, 'Openness is not a panacea. It will not suddenly teach students or spread "good" education, nor is it free of cultural baggage.' Both Boyle and Cormier are undoubtedly correct, and yet in the battle for openness, such critiques are often ignored. The danger of not addressing some of the issues around openness, however, is that they will be used to discredit the whole.

The Politics of Openness

In Chapter 2 I avoided giving a single definition of open education, because I wanted to admit degree and variation in practice. Whilst some areas, such as OERs, have a very clear definition, others such as open scholarship, represent a general approach and set of beliefs. Finding one definition would exclude some elements of the open education story that are interesting, hence the preference for a set of coalescing principles. This approach, however, does allow for vagueness in the term which potentially renders it meaningless, or subject to abuse.

In his thoughtful critique of open source publisher Tim O'Reilly, Morozov (2013) argues that this vagueness around the term has been deliberately constructed by O'Reilly to create good PR:

> Few words in the English language pack as much ambiguity and sexiness as 'open.' And after O'Reilly's bombastic interventions – 'Open allows experimentation. Open

encourages competition. Open wins,' he once proclaimed in an essay – its luster has only intensified. Profiting from the term's ambiguity, O'Reilly and his collaborators likened the 'openness' of open source software to the 'openness' of the academic enterprise, markets, and free speech. 'Open' thus could mean virtually anything.

For Morozov, O'Reilly's co-option of the term allowed him to ally it to economics, which the market found more palatable, allowing O'Reilly and many in the software movement to 'look political while advancing an agenda that had very little to do with politics'. As we saw in Chapter 1, openwashing suggests that there is market capital now in proclaiming open credentials, and ambiguity around the term facilitates this.

In Chapter 2, I set out a brief history of openness in education, but even this has political connotations. Such accounts of open education usually have one of two starting points. The first option is to take the founding of the Open University. Lane (2009) contends, 'The discourse around the role of openness in higher education can be said to have seriously started with the inception of the United Kingdom Open University (UKOU) in 1969.' The second, alternative, starting point for history is that of the open source movement, which is what Wiley and Gurell (2009) use, while admitting, 'Histories are difficult to write for many reasons. One reason is the difficulty of determining where to begin telling the story – for there is never a true starting point to a tale woven of people, events and ideas.' The choice of starting point will have an influence on the type of interpretation of open education put forward: the OU-based one may suggest a university and student focused approach, whereas the open source one might indicate a more technological and licence driven perspective.

Peter and Diemann (2013) propose a longer historical perspective, highlighting aspects of open education in the Middle Ages with the founding of universities which 'contained in them the idea of openness, albeit by no means comprehensive. This period highlights "open" as learner driven, resting on a growing curiosity and increasing awareness of educational opportunities.' Open education can be traced through the 17th century with coffeehouses and then into the industrial revolution with schools and working clubs. Their overview of this broader history of openness is shown in **Figure 9.**

This longer historical perspective has some illuminating lessons for the current debate. The authors conclude that, 'Historical forms of openness caution us against assuming that particular configurations will prevail, or that social aspects should be assumed as desired by default. ... After a period of open movements many times there have been slight but important shifts from "pure" openness towards "pretended" openness, i.e., some aspects have been modified to offer more control for producers and other stakeholders.'

This illustrates that openness has always been perceived as problematic, and one of its principle difficulties is that it operates against an individual's and, more significantly, an organisation's need to control. Where there are issues of control, there is undoubtedly a political aspect. Peters and Britez (2008) are blunt about this in their book on open education, opening with the statement, 'Open education involves a commitment to openness and is therefore inevitably a political and social project.' It is possible to argue, as the open source community do, that openness is simply the most efficient way to operate, and there is some truth in that, for instance the argument for learning objects and OERs makes this case. But even if that is so, a degree of politics follows.

Figure 9: A history of Openness.

Source: Peter & Deimann, 2013. Published under a CC-BY license.

This can be a set of assumed beliefs, in democracy, altruism, sharing or a general liberal perspective, or more directly, it can be political lobbying, for instance, to introduce open textbooks into a country or a region.

The political dimension of openness is perhaps best embodied in the story of Aaron Schwartz. A young programmer and online activist, Schwartz downloaded 19 million academic articles from the JSTOR database while at MIT, in order to make them freely available. He was indicted and charged with wire fraud and violation of the Computer Fraud and Abuse Act, which could have led to a penalty of US\$1 million in fines plus 35 years in prison. Schwartz committed suicide in January 2013. The case is a complicated one, as Schwartz did not distribute the articles and was not charged under copyright laws, but the severity of the potential punishment (although whether it would have ever been enforced is debatable) reinforces the claim that there are matters of real value being contested in the battle for openness. For some Schwartz is hero; for others he was 'reckless' (Aaronovitch 2013). Probably neither of these views is justified, but what this sad story does highlight is some of the issues that arise when open culture clashes with traditional practices. The relationship between the individual and their institution (some have criticised MIT for not protecting Schwartz), the adequacy of the law in dealing with these issues and the potential to easily distribute vast amounts of copyrighted material are all issues which will come up again. Schwartz's act can only be interpreted as a political one, however, and directly related to the issue of openness.

There have been explicitly political criticisms of aspects of open education. For instance MOOCs have been seen as exploiting academic labour (Zevin 2012) and of having a neoliberal agenda (Hall 2013). The Silicon Valley narrative can itself been seen as embodying a form of neoliberal capitalism, and so there should be no surprise that MOOCs can be seen from the same perspective. For others, the open education movement is not being radical enough in its reconceptualization of the role of universities. Winn (2012) asks, 'Is Open Education being used as a method of compensating for a decline in the welfare state? Is government advocacy of OER a way of tackling resource scarcity in an expanding system of higher education?' Winn and others favour a more social interpretation of openness, which draws on some of the historical trends mentioned above as well as the strong ethical basis of Stallman's free software movement. In this interpretation, open education leads to a cooperative university, which is 'a free association of people who come together to collectively produce knowledge. It is also a political project' (Winn 2013).

Even if one ignores such politically explicit aspects of open education, there is an unintentional (or maybe intentional) form of cultural imperialism associated with exporting the open education beliefs which are inextricably aligned with open education resources. Cormier (*2009*) suggests that OER can be viewed as a means of exporting an educational model. The power of a global institutional brand, such as MIT, combined with free (as in cost), makes it difficult for local providers to compete, both in terms of cost and voice. As Cormier puts it, 'How are local professors, debating the relative value of their curriculum against the standardizing power of a major university, going to be able to forward their own ideas?'

As with many of the criticisms in this chapter, there are arguments against this and means of mitigating against it, such as through localised projects, so it is not a reason in itself to hold against open education, but it should be acknowledged that a political dimension is present and alternatives may exist.

Problems with Openness

The previous section was concerned with philosophical or political reservations about open education. In this section some of the more specific problems associated with an open approach will be raised. This will not be an exhaustive list of such issues, but rather a representative one, with the intention of highlighting some of the problems that arise as a direct consequence of openness.

One of the most worrying problems associated with open education is that it isn't reaching the people it needs to, or claims to. As we have seen, much of the rhetoric for both OERs and MOOCs stresses the democratising nature of open approaches. While anecdotes are often used to back up this claim, the evidence does not support it. There seems to be a clear trend that the majority of users of open education material are those who are experienced learners already. For example a survey of users of the OU's OpenLearn OER repository found that it is often used by well-educated, well-qualified, employed informal and formal learners. For example, 26% of respondents indicated that they have undergraduate qualifications and a further 20% that they have postgraduate qualifications (Perryman, Law & Law 2013). Similarly the OpenCourseWare Consortium conducted a survey of users and found that nearly half were students currently undergoing secondary or university-level education, 22% were working professionals and 8% were teachers or faculty members (OCWC 2013). MOOCs exhibit similar learner demographics, with a study by Edinburgh University on the people using their six Coursera-based MOOCs showing that 70% of participants were qualified to undergraduate level or above (Edinburgh MOOC group 2013). Christensen et al. (2013) also found that across 32 MOOCs, learners tended to be young, white, educated, employed males.

Lane (2012) argues that it is not yet possible to measure how OERs are truly widening either formal or informal engagement in higher education but also suggests that most OERs are better suited to learners who are confident and experienced. Bossu, Bull and Brown (2012) indicate that, in the Australian context, those who most need access to higher education typically lack access to technology and, therefore, to OER. Liyanagunawardena, Williams and Adams (2013) express similar concerns regarding the potential of MOOCs to democratise education in developing countries, citing access to technologies, language and computer literacy as barriers, which may result in MOOCs serving only the privileged in developing countries.

Combined with accusations that MOOC providers are focusing on recruiting only elite universities (Rivard 2013), this certainly undermines the democratisation claim. Not only might open education not be reaching some of the target groups it aims for, but it could be exacerbating the situation. If independent study through MOOCs or OERs becomes a recognised desirable component on an individual's CV, then access to these may, ironically, increase the digital divide with experienced learners acquiring the benefits they offer.

Two drivers may mitigate against this scenario. The first is that these initial findings represent early stages in an adoption curve. It might be expected that experienced learners with high levels of connectivity would be amongst the first cohorts of a new development. As they become more accepted as part of the mainstream, then we would expect to see their uptake in broader society, in much the same way that Facebook moved from being a site used by a technological elite to a tool for the mass population.

The second driver is that global projects are taking much of the open ethos and applying it in a local context. For instance, the

TESSA project developed OERs for teacher education in Sub-Saharan Africa, with local contributors developing the material. The LatIN project is developing open textbooks for Latin America using local professors and authors, thus combating both the problems of cost and relevancy. Similarly, Siyavula in South Africa have developed open textbooks which are distributed nationally to all schools in key subjects. There are OER projects in most major countries, as the model of openness is seen as a means of addressing specific local needs.

Some of the response to these concerns, then, is that it is a developing picture, and it is unrealistic to expect an immediate resolution to problems of access that have plagued traditional education for a long time. The open education movement is being adapted and modified to meet the demands of local contexts. However, the learner profile is a concern, and the experience of open universities over the past 40 years has been that open entry students require a good deal of support. The 'build it and they will come' philosophy of some open education projects is unlikely to be sufficient in overcoming the barriers to participation for many learners. This emphasises the importance of maintaining a diversity of interpretations of openness and avoiding the simplistic 'open = free' definition, as open entry to learning may require different models of support.

A related aspect is the relatively low rates of reuse and adaptation of open content. Much is made of the 4 Rs of Reuse which we encountered in Chapter 2, but in reality only the first of these (the right to reuse something) is widely implemented. The others, revise, remix and redistribute, remain something of a minority interest. For instance, the OpenLearn team found that reversioning was rare, and users tended to take and deploy units wholesale. They found that repurposing material was avoided as a result of four main obstacles (McAndrew et al. 2009):

1. that it was not anyone's current role to remix and reuse;
2. the content provided on the site was of high quality and so discouraged alteration;
3. there were few examples showing the method and value of remixing;
4. the use of unfamiliar formats (such as XML) meant that users were uncertain how to proceed.

This suggests a mixture of cultural issues, such as a lack of defined roles, and technical ones acted as barriers to repurposing. As with the flipped learning network mentioned in Chapter 4, there was a disparity between teachers using others' material and then going on to share their own (De Los Arcos 2014). The picture may be changing, however. OpenStax statistics (from Jan 2014) show 361 derived versions of their textbooks from a total of 1,116 (OpenStax 2014). Some of these are different adaptations of the same module, so some modules are more likely to be repurposed than others, but it indicates a higher degree of adaptive reuse than we have seen in most OER projects. It may be that the familiar context of the OER in this case, a textbook rather than an elearning unit, overcomes some of the cultural and practice barriers, and the provision of easy tools for adaptation is similarly a factor.

All of this may not be significant; there will always be more straightforward reuse than adaptation, simply because the former is easier. Just as there are more YouTube consumers than producers, creating and sharing back content takes a greater commitment. However, for many open education practices to flourish, there needs to be a degree of community creation. I have made the distinction previously between big (i.e., institutional) and little (i.e., individual) OER (Weller 2012), but the same may be said of open scholarship, open access publishing and MOOCs. In part, this is an argument for sustainability; such approaches work well over a long period when they don't rely on large, centrally funded projects to deliver them, and instead they become a by-product of everyday practice. It is also an argument for ownership, which relates more specifically to the battle for open. If MOOCs are only developed through high-end productions featuring superstar academics, or if OERs are only delivered from large projects out of elite institutions and these are simply accepted wholesale, then academia does not take ownership of any of the issues or opportunities they offer. They remain a practice of others imposed upon the education sector, rather than one owned by it.

One other problem of open education is not lack of engagement, but over-zealous implementation. As discussed above, open education is undoubtedly a political movement, and as with any such movement, there are hardliners in its midst. These are often well intentioned and take a stance on openness that does not permit any of the reinterpetation of the term we see with openwashing. However, as with the open source movement, this can lead to a form of openness Stalinism, where people are outed for not being open enough. Ultimately this is alienating for many academics who don't want to be forced into open practice through fear or bullying. Openness can quickly become a stick with which to beat people, and the danger of this mindset is that openness is reduced to a narrow checklist. Perhaps the most exciting aspect of open practice is that it allows for experimentation and diversity, and it would be a false victory to replace one monopoly of behaviour with a new one.

Openness and access to a global network brings with it a new set of moral considerations. Openness can be used to justify behaviour. For example, is it acceptable to broadcast a quote or video of someone saying something offensive without their knowledge? Does a claim to openness justify public criticism of a lecturer? Many of these issues go beyond education, as society struggles to understand what it means for everyone to have access to a global network, when the consequences of actions became greatly amplified, as the Aaron Schwartz case reminds us. The 'Twitter storm' where an initial misdemeanour gains global attention and attracts a mob mentality is now commonplace. Often the original act is one that is genuinely offensive, such as the story of Justine Sacco who posted a racist joke before heading to South Africa and found herself dismissed from her job while in flight. While what she posted was undoubtedly crass, Wadhwa (2013) argues, 'At no point in history has it been so easy to destroy your entire life so quickly in so few words.' And while Sacco's indiscretion may have been genuinely distasteful, other cases occur through misunderstanding, as in the case of the teenage girl who joked that the world was 2,014 years old on New Year's Eve and received abuse, and even death threats from those who failed to appreciate the humour (Zimmerman 2014).

While Sacco and other Twitter morality outrages are based on unpleasant tweets, they are often no more offensive than the type of conversation one overhears in any public space. Someone won't have their life ruined for saying such things on a train or in a cafe, but if a television broadcaster said such things we would rightly be outraged by them. And this may indicate the difference we are now facing with our communication and our reactions – we are applying broadcast morality to personal communication.

There is sound advice for online behaviour, such as, 'treat everything you say online as broadcast', but any expression of humour or opinion may lead to a Twitter storm if it gets misconstrued.

The global, uncontrollable nature of such events puts the relationship between the individual academic and their institution under a new type of strain. Similarly, for academics who work in potentially sensitive subject areas, such as Middle-Eastern politics, climate change or evolutionary psychology, then pressure to be open and establish an online identity may subject them to particular groups with strong interests.

A further issue to consider with relation to openness is that of cost. Individuals often *overestimate* the time it takes to engage with tools such as blogs and social networking. While establishing an online identity does take some time, there is a period of investment, which has benefits once an identity has been established. Online networks can act as effective information filters, respondents to specific queries, research groupings for formal projects and dissemination routes, making it a time-saving practice. However, the cost of other aspects of openness may be *underestimated*. One example is that of open data. It may seem fairly trivial to release data for a particular project – whether this is through the project's own website, attached to a relevant publication or in a central repository. For many projects, in the hard sciences especially, this is the case – publicly sharing data from a collection of geology samples for instance. But as soon as human subjects are involved, data sharing becomes more complex. While it is easy to anonymise data, it turns out that deanonymisation is also not as difficult as one might imagine. In order to make any data that deals with people open, whether it is surveys, data records or interviews, researchers either need their consent to make it available as it is (a video interview for example), or they need to anonymise it. This involves removing identifiers such as name or student ID number. However, other pieces of data which are required for the data to be useful for researchers are also sufficient to allow for reidentification. In the US a person's date of birth, gender and zip code has been found to be unique for between 61% (Golle 2006) and 87% (Sweeney 2000) of the population. So to release this data requires considerable effort to make it truly anonymisable, and in order to do so, the reduction in the data quality may make releasing it worthless. Ohm (2009) concludes, 'Data can be either useful or perfectly anonymous but never both.'

These examples are used to illustrate that openness brings with it its own set of problems. One reaction to these types of challenges is often to withdraw, but that is to hand control over to others and for education and academics to be removed from the society in which they exist. Establishing the type of credible online identity discussed in the previous chapter is one element of this, but it will also require understanding and support from the institutions who have a relationship with those individuals.

Conclusions

As well as these issues, previous chapters of this book have raised other problems with the open approach, including:

- The Gold route for open access leading to unequal publishing opportunities
- Forcing students to adopt open behaviours that they may be uncomfortable with
- The low completion rates of MOOCs
- A route that permits increased commercialisation of education
- The long-term sustainability of OER projects

Each of the issues raised in this overview arises because of the open nature of the practice, and in addition there will be other related issues which impinge upon open education, such as the costs associated with higher education. This highlights that open education, as well as offering solutions to some issues, brings with it a new set of concerns, which need to be addressed. The severity and impact of these problems is not clear. Some may be attributed to open education still being relatively new, and changes in practice take time to establish themselves. Awareness of online resources has greatly increased over the past decade, although often it is confined to popular sites such as YouTube, iTunes U, and TED talks. This is likely to continue over the next decade, and reusing content will become more of an accepted part of practice. Similarly, awareness of rights and the desire to remix will increase, simply because of a growing general awareness in society. The use of social media and everyday acts of sharing photos and videos already means it is a far more commonplace practice than it was even five years ago.

Institutional awareness of open practice has increased dramatically, and here some credit must be given to the role that MOOCs have played in this. MOOCs have dramatically increased the level of attention to open practice, which always carries with it some negative results as well as the positive.

This chapter illustrates that we should not think of openness as a simple checklist, but in allowing a broader definition the opportunities for misuse increase, either for commercial reason, as in openwashing, or to justify questionable behaviour. One way of thinking about open educational practice is what Kelty (2008) terms 'recursive publics', which he defines as, 'a public that is constituted by a shared concern for maintaining the means of association through which they come together as a public.' This concept was used to examine how free software computer hackers cooperate and behave in a highly functional community, without recourse to a clearly defined manifesto or constitution. Kelty argues that they are operating in the public domain, and at the same time that is altering their own behaviour, so an evolving definition of what it means to be a hacker is being developed. The core values of these hackers hold them together, but they are simultaneously creating the context within which they operate. As Winn (2013) suggests, this notion can be applied to open education also, which is both 'in and against' a particular context. As we saw in the previous chapter on identity, open scholars can be seen as defining themselves both within their current discipline and institution, but also acting in contrast to many of those practices. This needn't be a confrontational 'against', but rather one of highlighting relevant contrast. Open access publishing is not against publishing, after all, but it defines itself by highlighting crucial elements of difference. This concept of defining open practice as being simultaneously within and against current educational practice gives rise to much of the tension that has been identified in previous chapters. In the next chapter we will look at a method of framing these tensions and considering an individual or institution's ability to deal with them.

CHAPTER 9

Resilience and Open Education

None are so anxious as those who watch and wait.
—Charles Dickens

Introduction

In previous chapters the victory of the open approach has been considered, as well as the areas that now constitute the battle for open. Chapter 6 argued that the battle for narrative played a significant role in the larger battle, and that it was often dominated by simplistic demands for revolution and disruption. In this chapter, a framework for considering these tensions is proposed, and one which offers an alternative narrative for considering the changes that openness brings to education. Chapter 6 highlighted a paradox for many in the open education movement: how to emphasise the possibilities and potential that openness brings to education without resorting to calls for the wholesale overthrow of the education system itself, which many of those adopting the 'open' label deem necessary. The 'education is broken' stance demands that change occurs only once complete revolution has taken place, and it forces people to take extreme positions for and against.

By offering an alternative narrative, the aim of this chapter is to demonstrate that this revolution approach is not the only way to consider changes in higher education. The framework suggested here is that of resilience, but its function is illustrative, to demonstrate that alternative narratives and conceptualisations are possible. Resilience offers a tool for considering both the current context and areas that need addressing if an individual or an institution is to meet the challenges of open education. It is adapted from the notion of resilience in ecology, and I proposed it as a possible model at the end of *The Digital Scholar* (2011). This chapter extends that work, and, as well as the practical approach for considering the impact of any particular open education approach, the use of resilience to offer a narrative for considering changes to the education system as a whole is proposed.

Resilience

The concept of resilience has been applied in many domains, but has its roots in Holling's (1973) study on the stability of ecological systems. The definition of resilience used was 'a measure of the persistence of systems and of their ability to absorb change and disturbance and still maintain the same relationships between populations or state variables.' Resilience has found favour as a way of considering climate change. Hopkins (2009) defined it as 'the capacity of a system to absorb disturbance and reorganise while undergoing change, so as to retain essentially the same function, structure, identity and feedbacks.' Walker et al. (2004) propose four aspects of resilience, which will form the basis of the approach used in this chapter:

1. Latitude: the maximum amount a system can be changed before losing its ability to recover.
2. Resistance: the ease or difficulty of changing the system; how 'resistant' it is to being changed.
3. Precariousness: how close the current state of the system is to a limit or 'threshold'.
4. Panarchy: the influences of external forces at scales above and below. For example, external oppressive politics, invasions, market shifts or global climate change can trigger local surprises and regime shifts.

Using these factors, resilience provides a useful means of considering the response of scholars and institutions to the potential impact of open education. The emphasis in this consideration is on retaining function, not just 'resisting' change. Taleb (2012) has argued that the perspective should move beyond resilience and consider 'antifragility', stating, 'The antifragile is beyond the resilient or robust. The resilient resists shocks and stays the same; the antifragile gets better and better.' This is to equate resilience with resistance. Indeed, a high resistance is not necessarily a benefit to an ecosystem, as Holling observed; for example, some insect populations fluctuate wildly depending on environmental factors but prove to be resilient over time. Resilience requires adaptation and evolution to new environmental conditions but retains core identity. In ecosystems this means the species persists, although it may be adapted, and in organisational terms it means the core functions remain, although they may be realised in newer (and in Taleb's view, better) ways.

In terms of open education practice, resilience is about utilising the open approach where this is desirable but retaining the underlying function and identity that the existing practices represent, if they are still deemed to be necessary. The practices themselves are not core to scholarship; rather, they are the methods through which core functions are realised, and these methods can and should change. The peer-review process in academic publishing, for example, is a method of ensuring quality, objectivity and reliability. But it may not be the only or the best way of realising this, as we have seen, and open education may allow different forms of it to be realised. A resilience perspective would seek to ensure these core functions were protected, and not just resist at the level of the method.

Although resilience can be seen at the individual level, it is perhaps best applied to the institutional level, which can be seen as a complex ecosystem in itself, comprised of a number of individuals, behaviours and tasks. The resilience approach will now be considered for a case study at the Open University.

In this approach, Walker's four aspects of resilience will be considered, and a score allocated against each aspect to provide an indicative measure of overall resilience. Each factor is given a subjective ranking of 1 to 10 (1 = low resilience, 10 = high resilience). A high score of more than 35 would indicate that it is probably not a particularly new challenge (or that the institution was exceptionally well adapted already), and a low score of less than 15 would indicate that the institution faces a considerable threat from this challenge, which it has not adapted to.

The Open University and MOOCs

In order to demonstrate the utility of the resilience model, one of the main developments we have seen in previous chapters will be considered – namely, MOOCs. The impact of these will be considered for the UK Open University to provide an illustrative example.

As we have seen, there has been considerable hype and over-promise concerning MOOCs, but they represent a good example for analysis in terms of resilience for a number of reasons. Firstly, they are a new practice which could only practically have been realised in a digital, networked, open context. As we saw in the more detailed history of open education set out in the previous chapter, free, open education has been attempted before, but it was limited by physical and geographical constraints – only so many people could attend a lecture hall, and correspondence formats lacked interactive and mediated variety and appeal. By contrast, open online courses are available to everyone with an internet connection, and beyond certain server restrictions, it makes no difference if more students sign up. The second reason they make a good case study is that they propose both a threat and opportunity to standard education practice, at least in the eyes of many participants. They are not therefore a niche interest, limited to only a specific discipline, culture or geographical region. Thirdly, they are present in increasing numbers now, and while some may make predictions (both positive and negative) about their future growth, there are sufficient numbers and interest to examine them today. They are not based on a possible model of what might or could happen, but a functional one that is occurring now. Daniel (2013) suggests that although we have seen other ventures disappear, MOOCs are likely to persist and they 'will have an important impact in two ways: improving teaching and encouraging institutions to develop distinctive missions.' They are therefore an ideal case study for resilience.

For the Open University, MOOCs represent both a challenge and an opportunity. As a purely distance-education institution it is arguably more vulnerable to their threat. If learners can study for free, the argument goes, then why would they pay for an education that isn't campus based?

In December 2012 the OU announced the launch of FutureLearn, a separate company founded by the OU, in consortium with a range of UK universities to provide MOOCs on a global platform. This represents a significant investment in terms of resources, finances and brand in MOOCs, which highlights their resonance with the OU's core functions.

Taking the four resilience perspectives offers a means and a lens for both assessing this risk and highlighting potential courses of action.

Latitude

The OU developed a model of distance learning based around primarily printed units and accompanying media (be it television programmes, audio cassettes or DVDs), supported by a tutor or associate lecturer. This is the Supported Open Learning (SOL) model, which Jones et al. (2009) summarise as being based on three key factors:

1. Distance or Open Learning
   a. Learning 'in your own time'
   b. Reading, undertaking set activities and assignments
   c. Possibility but not compulsion to work with others
2. Resources
   a. Printed course materials, assigned textbooks, audio and video cassettes, CD/DVD materials, home experiments, course and program websites (previously broadcast TV programs)

3. Systematic support
   a. An assigned course tutor, a regional network of centres, central library student and technical support
   b. Tutorials held within regions, day schools and online (e.g. languages, summer schools)

The advent of elearning in the late 1990s saw an adaptation of this model, but not a fundamental shift. Bell and Lane (1998) describe how the implementation of ICT into the existing distance-education model could be seen as combining the strengths of the traditional campus and distance modes. The OU introduced home computers in 1988 and implemented a large-scale elearning course in 1999 (Weller & Robinson, 2002). This demonstrates that its core SOL model has not been so rigid that it cannot adapt and that it is robust enough to survive new models of implementation. The OU, then, has a reasonable degree of latitude, in that it has a history of adapting its model to accommodate new technology and practices.

With MOOCs, the degree of latitude required is still uncertain. The current MOOC model is unsupported (or mainly peer supported) and free of cost to the students. This highlights a conflict with the OU's core SOL model, which posits human, tutor support as a core element, and which inevitably incurs a cost. As was set out in Chapter 5, the cost of this support is the most significant element in the lifetime of a course. Kop (2011) notes that learners in MOOCs:

> have to be confident and competent in using the different tools in order to engage in meaningful interaction. It takes time for people to feel competent and comfortable to learn in an autonomous fashion, and there are critical literacies … that are prerequisites for active learning in a changing and complex learning environment without the provision of too much organized guidance by facilitators.

For many of the learners that the OU traditionally engages with, developing these literacies through the supported model is a key function of the educational process. Furthermore, those who are challenged in their progress or capacity to attain these competencies have a variety of scaffolds and support services to draw upon at the OU. With MOOCs the options are largely limited to withdrawing from the course or seeking peer support.

Resistance

The OU is a large institution, with over 250,000 students and 11,000 employees. As such, it has been required to develop well-defined processes for dealing with scale, for example in assignment handling, tutor allocation and student support. Inevitably, large-scale systems are more difficult to adapt than small-scale ones, just as large companies are less adaptable than small, agile ones. The OU has developed a production model which was initially focused around print but has and continues to adapt to the different cost demands of elearning (Bates 1995).

Changing such systems is possible, but it requires strategic direction and leadership and is not done quickly. Success depends on the degree of adaptation required. MOOCs appear to require many of the systems already in place; for example, the IT infrastructure for dealing with large student numbers, elearning content that is designed to be studied independently, methods for informal assessment, etc. The work done previously for OERs in OpenLearn specifically, and elearning in general, lays a foundation that means MOOCs are technically feasible. The broader issues – such as ensuring a good student experience when there is no tutor present and implementing methods of informal assessment (such as Mozilla badges) and how these relate to official accreditation, raising issues for a large-scale institution with a global brand – are more difficult. In terms of resistance, then, the OU is well placed, in that it has adaptable infrastructure, but susceptible in that it arguably has greater potential for damage to its brand than a smaller institution.

It is the examination of this factor that reveals the OU's solution to MOOCs in FutureLearn most clearly. The OU has the infrastructure systems required to support large-scale, high-quality MOOCs, but not the small nimble approach required for more experimental versions. A solution that meets these strengths combines elements of both the expertise and scale of the existing organisation, with the agility required of a small start-up. FutureLearn therefore represents a model which most conveniently plays to the OU's strengths and renders resistance less of a consideration.

Precariousness

With 246,626 registered students in 2012 and a £252M reserve (Open University 2012), the OU is not in an immediately precarious state, although both of these figures may be negatively affected by changes in the student fee structure as set out below. MOOCs have arrived at a time of great upheaval in the UK higher education system, with the introduction of student fees. This is dealt with in more detail in the next section under panarchy, as it represents an external force.

It has necessitated wholesale change in the model used by the OU, both in terms of funding and course delivery. Student fees are associated with a qualification and not with individual modules, requiring a shift in the granularity of operation to this higher level. This has required the types of large, systemic institutional changes mentioned above, which are possible but inevitably time consuming, often personally challenging and a drain on resources. Arguably, then, this external influence has forced changes that have meant less attention and resource could be allocated to MOOC experimentation than might have been possible in previous eras.

A sudden, and large-scale defection of learners to MOOCs away from formal study would be precarious for the OU; however, this does not appear to be imminent. Indeed, it could be argued that MOOCs and formal education are complementary to one another, as MOOCs lead to low-risk engagement from learners, a proportion of which is then realised as formal study. A range of strategic analyses of MOOCs have been conducted at the OU (e.g. Sharples et al. 2012), from a pedagogic, technical and commercial perspective, which suggest that precariousness is not a major factor at this particular time, although there is a possibility for MOOCs to have an impact upon core business in the future. FutureLearn is seen as a deliberate attempt to reduce any threat of precariousness by owning a strategic, political solution to MOOCs.

Panarchy

The influence of external forces is particularly relevant in this period, with a global financial crisis, an ongoing European crisis and changes in the higher education funding model in the UK. All of these factors may lead to a decline in the number of students entering and remaining in higher education programs. They probably also account for much of the interest in MOOCs, with open courses being proposed as a solution to the problem of costly higher education (e.g. Kamenetz 2010).

As mentioned, the changes in funding structure have necessitated large-scale institutional change at the OU, combined with a need to increase student fees to compensate for the loss of state funding. This may well result in different student demographics (for example, a decline in leisure learners, but an increase in full-time students who find the OU a cheaper option than campus students), although it is too early in the process to assess these impacts.

MOOCs therefore enter the market at a time of great uncertainty, when panarchic effects are high for the OU (and all UK universities). This may account for the more cautious response from UK universities (Fazackerley 2012) compared with that in North America.

This analysis can be summarised in a subjective scoring, allocating a score of 1 (weak resilience) to 10 (strong resilience) for each of the four factors. A score of 20 or lower would indicate an overall susceptibility to this particular digital factor, but it will also highlight individual areas of weakness. For the Open University, such a scoring is set out in **Table 1**.

Resilience factor	Score	Comments
Latitude	8	Based on ability and history of adapting to technological change
Resistance	8	Large institution with established systems and high reputation risk, solution plays to strengths
Precariousness	7	Not immediate, but comes in time of change and has direct relevance to OU model
Panarchy	6	UK subject to considerable upheaval in higher education sector
Total	29	An area of concern, but resources and practices allow adaptation. Dealing with large-scale systems and the impact of UK sector changes are priorities for reinforcing resilience

Table 1: Resilience factors for MOOCs for the UK Open University.

The score of 29 indicates that MOOCs represent a challenge to the OU, but one which it is developing resilient practices to meet.

Adaptive Cycles

Walker and Salt (2006) apply resilience thinking to economic scenarios as well as ecological ones, for instance, as a model to consider the changing fortunes of a construction company or the nature of a town over time. Key to their model is the adaptive cycle, which Gunderson and Holling (2002) observed in ecological systems. This has four main phases: rapid growth, conservation, release and reorganization, as illustrated in **Figure 10**.

Rapid growth is the initial expansion (of a business or a population), conservation is when it maintains a steady state, release is a period of 'creative destruction', when it enters a new phase, and reorganisation is when it re-establishes itself in a new state.

For Walker and Salt, a system can have many different stable states, separated by thresholds. When a system crosses a threshold,

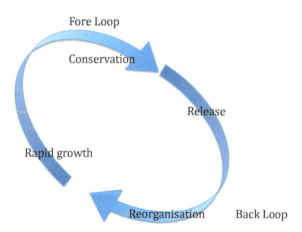

Figure 10: The adaptive cycle. [adapted from Walker & Salt 2006]

it enters a different state. Resilience then can be viewed as the distance from a threshold. Taking our example above, one way of interpreting the anxiety or hype around MOOCs is that they are proposed as a factor that could push universities into a different state (one where they cease to exist in some scenarios, or radically alter their business models). In this interpretation, one could argue that universities have successfully maintained the conservation phase for the past 200 years or so. Walker and Salt propose that an end to the conservation phase is inevitable and that 'The longer the conservation phase persists the smaller the shock needed to end it.'

Rapid growth and conservation represent the 'fore loop' in the adaptive cycle, when a system is maturing, but it is inevitably followed by the back loop of release and reorganisation. Is open education the 'small shock' required to cross the transition for universities into the release phase?

As they suggest, it is important to look across scales, not at one level of granularity, so maybe the university, or 'education' is the wrong level to focus on. Higher education is a complex, multi-faceted offering, comprising teaching, research and social function. Rather than view it as one system, it is perhaps better viewed as a combination of smaller, interconnected ones. In this view, openness may well act as the release and reorganisation of a particular element within a university or the system as a whole. For example, publishing is one element of the overall academic system, and here the advent of open access could be seen to be pushing the existing system into release mode. This is a period where new models are developed, existing companies and roles are altered, and it enters a reorganisation phase. What will emerge then is a very different type of academic publishing system.

The battle for open could be conceived as the necessary perturbations that occur during this 'back loop'. In Chapter 2, it was suggested that it is now a question of which type of openness one wanted, rather than simply open vs. closed. One way of thinking of this is to see it as a number of smaller resilience transitions occurring, where the common theme is an open approach as the cause of the shift. But the overall system (that of education) may still be resilient, in the same way that a number of smaller forest fires may occur but at a national level the forestry retains its resilience. This shift in granularity allows us to observe the significant changes that open education is creating without recourse to the wholesale 'revolution' or 'disruption' required by the mindset seen in Chapter 7.

Levels of OER Engagement

To illustrate how this approach offers an alternative narrative for open education, let us consider OERs and the different levels of engagement people have with them. Open education in general, and OERs specifically, form a basis from which many other practices benefit, but often practitioners in those areas are unaware of OERs explicitly. It is likely that these secondary and tertiary levels of OER awareness represent a far greater audience than the primary 'OER-aware' one, so one can view the sizes of these audiences like the metaphorical iceberg, with increasing size as one goes into these unseen areas. There are three possible areas of OER usage:

Primary OER usage – This group is 'OER aware', in that the term itself will have meaning for them; they are engaged with issues around open education; they are aware of open licences and they are often advocates for OERs. This group has often been the focus of OER funding, conferences and research, with the focus on growing the ranks of this audience. An example would be a community college teacher who adopts and contributes to open textbooks.

Secondary OER usage – This group may have some awareness of OERs or open licences, but they have a pragmatic approach to them. OERs are of secondary interest to their primary task, usually teaching. OERs (and openness in general) can be seen as the substratum which allows some of their practice to flourish, but they are not aware or interested in open education itself as a topic, rather their own subject is of prime interest, and therefore OERs are only of interest to the extent that they facilitate innovation or efficiency in this. An example of this group might be a 'flipped learning' teacher who uses Khan academy, TED talks and some OERs in their teaching.

Tertiary OER usage – this group will use OERs amongst a mix of other media and often not differentiate between them. Awareness of licences is low and not a priority. OERs are a 'nice to have' option but not essential, and users are often largely consuming rather than creating and sharing. An example would be a student studying at university who uses iTunes U materials to supplement their taught material.

David Wiley (2009) has talked of Dark Reuse – that is, whether reuse is happening in places we can't observe (analogous to dark matter) or simply isn't happening much at all. He poses the challenge to the OER movement about its aims:

> If our goal is catalyzing and facilitating significant amounts of reuse and adaptation of materials, we seem to be failing. …
>
> If our goal is to create fantastically popular websites loaded with free content visited by millions of people

each month, who find great value in the content but never adapt or remix it, then we're doing fairly well.

By considering these three levels of OER engagement, it is possible to see how both elements of Wiley's goals are realisable. The main focus of OER initiatives has often been the primary OER usage group. Here OERs are created and there are OER advocacy missions. For example, Wild (2012) suggests three levels of engagement for HE staff that progress from piecemeal to strategic to embedded use of OER. The implicit assumption is that one should encourage progression through these levels; that is, the route to success for OERs is to increase the population of the primary OER group.

Whilst this is undoubtedly a good thing to do (assuming one believes in the benefits of OERs), it may not be the only approach. Another approach may be to increase penetration of OERs into the secondary and tertiary levels. Awareness of OER repositories was very low amongst this group, compared with resources such as the Khan Academy or TED. The focus on improving uptake for these groups is then to increase visibility, search engine optimisation and convenience of the resources themselves, without knowledge of open education. This might be realised through creating a trusted brand to compete with resources such as TED.

To apply the resilience model to this model of OER usage, it could be proposed that we have been through the rapid-growth stage for primary OER usage, and this has entered the conservation stage now. There is an accepted, stable community and approach. However, in order for OERs to reach the secondary users, it needs to enter a new phase of release. This is usually achieved through some period of creative destruction. One might argue that the impact of MOOCs on the OER community could be seen as such a force, pushing them into a new state, or that a change in funding and direction is required to create such a change.

The useful perspective this offers is that it is not about wholesale change and debunking of a previous approach, but moving from one state to another. Such a view allows greater continuity between developments in education than the Silicon Valley narrative permits.

Conclusion

The resilience model in ecology offers a model for considering how adept a system is at absorbing change. It thus offers a useful model for analysing an institution's ability to adapt within an altered environment, while retaining its core functionality. It is not without its critics or difficulties, however. One should always exercise caution as to the extent an analogy with the natural world can be applied to sociological constructs such as education. Like disruption, it could also be seen to be advancing a neoliberal agenda, and one could certainly contest Walker and Salt's conclusion that the end of the conservation stage is always inevitable. It does, however, serve three purposes in the consideration of the battle for open. Firstly, it provides a framework for analysing any particular impact, as with the MOOCs example above; secondly, it offers a means of considering individual areas of impact within the larger system; and lastly, it suggests that other narratives apart from the dominant Silicon Valley one are possible.

Considering the first of these functions, the model can be used as a qualitative analysis tool to highlight areas of concern and to help set priorities. The scoring method set out in this chapter is one method of achieving this, but there are no correct scores; these will be subjective. The methodology was conducted with a wider group of eight participants at the OU. Scores ranged from 23 to 32, but there was general consensus around the relevant issues and responses.

Applying the method for the same open education challenge (MOOCs) at a different university will reveal differences in factors such as preparedness, national contexts, student demographics, etc. Analysis of a different open education challenge, such as open access publishing, at the same university will highlight factors such as the degree of impact, the maturity of the challenge, area of impact, etc.

As a framework for analysing the impact of a particular change wrought by new technology, however, the metaphor provides a means of identifying strengths and weaknesses and articulating responses. It also provides a framework for considering the different aspects of openness as being connected into part of a larger whole while maintaining the integrity of that larger system. As Walker and Salt argue, 'There is a much higher likelihood of crossing a threshold into a new regime if you are unaware of its existence,' so an appreciation of the impact of open education may be the best method for maintaining resilience.

CHAPTER 10

The Future of Open

There is no time-out in [Keith Moon's] drumming because there is no time-in. It is all fun stuff.

—James Wood

Introduction

In this concluding chapter I will revisit some of the themes of this book and attempt to make the case for why openness really matters in the future of education. I will also set out some recommendations for considering open education in the short to medium term.

In chapter 1, I made the claim that openness has been victorious in many respects, and this was reinforced by examining the success of open access publishing, OERs, MOOCs and open scholarship. However, to many working in higher education, this would seem a rather overblown claim. They may work in contexts where open scholarship is not only not recognised, but actively discouraged, where the mention of OERs would be met with blank expressions and any proposed change to take advantage of the opportunities of open education is actively resisted. Any notion that openness has won seems like the fancy of a privileged few, perhaps operating within an open education bubble.

I have sympathy with this view, so before we progress it is worth revisiting this claim and clarifying it somewhat. During the course of this book, I have set out many examples that I think demonstrate the success of the open approach: the open access mandates: the numbers of learners and media interest in MOOCs; the impact and sustainability of open textbooks; and the changing nature of fundamental scholarly practice as a result of open approaches. To suggest that openness has been successful is not to claim that it has achieved saturation or 100% uptake. Rather it is that all of these separate successes point to a larger trend – this is the moment when openness has moved from being a peripheral, specialist interest to a mainstream approach. To use that oft-quoted (and perhaps meaningless) term, it is at a tipping point. From this moment, the application of open approaches in all aspects of higher education practice has both legitimacy and a certain inevitably. This is not to say that it will always be adopted, just as the open source approach to software is not always pursued, but it is an increasingly pervasive method. The speed of acceptance will be influenced by a number of factors, such as disciplinary cultures, national programmes, policies, funding, the presence of champions and immediate benefits.

The victory of open education, then, is that it is now a serious contender, proposed by more than just its devoted acolytes as a method for any number of higher education initiatives, be they in research, teaching or public engagement. This transition is at the heart of this book, since inherent in it are opportunities and challenges, just as a small start-up business must face a whole different set of issues when it grows and becomes a larger multi-national corporation. In this transition there are many potential pitfalls – the whole enterprise can fail, it can be taken over by others or the fundamental value and identity that characterised that embryonic stage can be lost.

Open Policy

One aspect of this transition is that it moves from informal to formal practice. One form this will take is the increase in policies relating to open educational practice. These can be at a national, regional, funder, institutional or departmental level and can address different aspects of practice, such as open access publishing, release of open data, academic profiles online, release of open education materials and so on.

Given this wide variation in what constitutes an open education policy, it is difficult to chart their uptake. The ROARMAP project at Southampton University records open access policies at funder, institutional and sub-institutional level, while Creative Commons hosts a registry of OER-related policies (Creative Commons 2013b) and the OER Research Hub (2014) maps all such policies.

The POERUP project has been examining OER policies in depth and highlights the complex nature of the field (Bacsich 2013). In the US, there are a growing number of state or school policies, but these are often targeted exclusively at the provision of open textbooks, largely with cost savings as a driving factor. This form of OER is less prevalent in Europe. In addition, there are policies which may have a strong influence on open education but which are not directly open education policies themselves. For instance, agreed systems of assessing prior learning and acknowledging informal learning would aid the adoption of OERs and MOOCs, without explicitly being OER policies.

There are two rather conflicting messages from this work, which can be seen as representative of the broader state that open education finds itself in. On the positive side, there is evidence of a growing number of policies that are directly or indirectly related to open education. Open access policies are perhaps the most obvious of these, but these have been followed by policies regarding open data (i.e., that not only should publications arising from public funding be made openly available, but the experimental data should also) and open textbooks. This indicates a succession model, wherein once one element is open then it follows that others should be also (this is explored below). From this perspective, open policy looks like it might well be the next major breakthrough for the open education movement, and as such, it will mark a significant point in its transition into the mainstream.

However as Bacsich as well as Farrow and Frank-Bristow (2014) suggest, it is currently a very mixed area, with different types of policy, and at the OER level, often a lack of substantial policy. Often an OER project is undertaken by a specific project within a university, and once that funding finishes, the project ceases. Farrow and Frank-Bristow suggest that policy forms part of a formula that is often seen with successful OER projects, which requires a pilot study, funding, a champion and policy to achieve sustainability and substantial impact. Unless such a sustainable model is established with senior management commitment, many projects do not lead to an OER policy being adopted by the institution. Developing a policy that relates to OER is crucial for the longevity of such policies, but too often it is not expressed as an explicit goal, and thus the project rather fizzles out for want of a strategic direction. As open education moves into the next phase, policies should be seen as not only a driver for this, but also an aim; the explicit intention to establish such a policy should form part of an open education project.

The Lesson from the LMS

The open policy example gives a broader indication as to the response that educators need to take to openness if it is to continue to be successful and meet their needs. We can also look at a recent example which offers a cautionary tale to help inform this direction. This is the Learning Management System (LMS), or the Virtual Learning Environment (VLE).

In the late 1990s elearning was seen as a novel approach to education. It was subject to much of the same promise, hype and anxiety that we now see with MOOCs. It could variously offer a cheap way of providing education (Noam 1995), make lecturers redundant (Noble 1998), provide a route to innovative ways of teaching (Weller 2002) or remove the barrier of distance (Mason 2000). While many in education embraced the possibilities of elearning by adopting innovative pedagogies and using a range of media and tools, there was reluctance and resistance from many. A combination of the perceived efficiency benefits, flexibility for learners and ability to reach new audiences meant that elearning was soon on the agenda of most senior managers in universities.

The early stages of elearning adoption were often characterised by a mixed economy of technologies, with different departments adopting different systems, usually driven by champions and early adopters. The early '00s saw an inevitable consolidation phase; the maintenance of so many disparate systems became problematic and, in order to gain the perceived benefits of elearning, a uniform approach was required. This is when the LMS became a dominant solution, for instance, in the UK by 2003, 86% of higher education institutions had one (Brown and Jenkins 2003). The LMS provided a convenient suite of tools, and with a standard system, it allowed universities to implement staff development programmes and allowed for students to have access to consistent technology. All of this facilitated the uptake of elearning, and if one was a champion of such an approach, it could be viewed as a positive advancement. The LMS was the key to elearning becoming a mainstream approach.

However, there were two unfortunate side effects to the widescale adoption of LMSs. The first was that academia often outsourced the technology and also the approach to elearning. By adopting commercial systems such as Blackboard, they gained a robust and quick solution, but they often lost the expertise or the control required to innovate in this area. Such relationships were not always mutually beneficial either, such as when Blackboard attempted to impose patent rights to generic elearning requirements such as tutor group formation (Geist 2006).

The second issue was largely a function of the first: rather than being a stepping stone to further elearning experimentation, the LMS became an end point in itself. As institutional processes came into place, they created a sediment around the system, so the question was no longer one of 'what can we do with elearning?' but rather one of 'what do I need to do with the LMS to meet the university requirement?' The online classroom model, or using the LMS as a repository for lecture notes, came to be seen as elearning itself, and further experimentation often ceased. This demonstrates the importance of policy in establishing uptake, but also of allowing a policy that has sufficient room within it to allow for innovation.

Groom and Lamb (2014) see the LMS as the prime suspect in a loss of innovation around elearning in universities. Their case against the LMS has five main points:

- Systems – The LMS privileges a technology management mindset.

- Silos – The artificially closed and protected environment of the LMS does not allow for the benefits of openness.
- Missed opportunities – Learners use a system that is unlike anything outside of education and spend their time learning to use the LMS itself.
- Costs – LMSs drain the financial and also the human resources, so there is little capacity to support any innovation outside of the system. In essence the LMS becomes the answer to all elearning problems.
- Confidence – there is a lack of enthusiasm for LMSs, and educational technologists who might otherwise be undertaking innovative work are required to manage the system, leading to a loss in confidence to experiment beyond this.

Referring to the manner in which universities often eschew innovative use of the internet in teaching, Groom (2014) sums it up, claiming, 'In a depressing twist of fate, higher ed has outsourced the most astounding innovation in communications history that was born on its campuses.' The resonance with open education is very strong; one could almost substitute commercial MOOCs for LMSs in the above and the same would be true. This recent history illustrates the potential danger in allowing control and direction of open education to be determined by external parties. Universities too quickly become the consumers of this solution rather than the driving force behind it.

Education Challenges

Having looked at one possible area of open education progression in policy and the importance of involvement and ownership regarding the future direction of open education, we will now revisit the value of the open approach, to reinforce the significance of engaging with open education. In Chapter 2, I listed some of the possible motivations for adopting an open approach at an individual level. In this section, the possible benefits of openness as a solution to the broader challenges facing education will be outlined.

One issue for universities is the justification of their social relevance. In a digital age, what is the role of the university? In a world of Wikipedia and Google, why do people need to go to a university to study for three years or more? One only has to look at the comments section of any newspaper article about universities to see such views expressed. They are often perceived as being ivory towers, behind the times or out of touch. Of course, one can easily counter such arguments, stressing the quality and depth of a university education, the critical skills that are developed, as well as the social function of universities. The problem is not that claims regarding the irrelevance of universities can be refuted, but that they become commonly accepted beliefs, regardless of evidence. As we saw in the chapter on the Silicon Valley narrative, once myths become pervasive, they are difficult to counter.

The solution open education offers here is to easily demonstrate all of the aspects of higher education that might be championed as worthwhile. If it is the quality of resources, then OERs can reveal why there is depth beyond the Wikipedia article. If it is about research, then open access articles demonstrate the value of in-depth research that is not commercially funded and biased. Open scholarship highlights that individual academics are not operating in isolation and are engaged with the broader community and implications. A practical example is provided by Oregon State University library. Just as the question of relevance is raised for universities, so the role of libraries in the digital age is also under examination. The OSU library, in collaboration with their own university press, is working with academics to create open textbooks for undergraduates (OSU 2014). This is mainly aimed at addressing the issue of cost for students, but it also enhances the university's reputation, as these books are open to all, and increases student satisfaction, as the material can be adapted to suit the changing needs of curriculum. University libraries are perfectly positioned to perform this function with all the requisite skills and resources, and it arguably offers a better return on investment than procuring access to journals which are read by only a small group of researchers.

All of these forms of openness are relatively easy to realise and aim at simply exposing the good practice within universities. In a digital, networked age, erecting boundaries around the institution is harmful because it speaks of isolation.

A related issue is the suitability of the learning experience in the world the graduate will encounter when they leave education. It is a frequent complaint that graduates are not suitably equipped with the skills they need for employment (e.g. Levy 2013). It's possible that this claim is ill-founded and rather it is that employers may not be equipped to deal with the modern skill set their graduates possess. However, if there is validity in it, then open practice again provides a partial solution. To revisit one of the objections of Groom and Lamb, the LMS, and indeed the university physical environment, is one that is largely unlike any other. Too often assessment and coursework focuses on artificial tasks or contrived examples. Open practice allows students to engage in the type of tasks and develop the type of skills they may need in any type of employment, without reducing a university education to merely vocational training. For instance, establishing an online identity and blogging for an open audience requires the development of communication skills beyond a narrow focus. Editing Wikipedia articles necessitates engagement with a process of evidence gathering and collaboration. Creating YouTube videos requires creativity and the ability to learn skills independently, and so forth. This is not to suggest that all university education is conducted in the open; there are valuable reasons behind nurturing confidence in a closed environment. But I would suggest that the development of the skills required to operate in the open internet are more likely to provide employers with attributes that are useful to them than a purely 'closed' model of education.

Underlying these two concerns is often one of cost. Given the high price of a university degree (whether it is funded by the state or the individual student), are there cheaper alternatives available? Does the university model still represent the best value for money? This promise of cheaper education was one of the drivers behind elearning and the enthusiasm for MOOCs. It is rarely borne out, though; the cost of producing elearning courses was not as cheap as many envisaged, and as we saw in Chapter 5, MOOC financial models are far from stable.

So claims about dramatic cost reductions should be treated with some scepticism. What open education can do effectively, however, is influence related factors. For example, creating a course using a wide range of good-quality OERs will reduce the amount of bespoke material that is required. This may reduce the time required to produce the course or provide a higher-quality course for the same investment. As we saw in the discussion on OERs, they are frequently used by students prior to study or while engaged in formal education. This may reduce the number of students who take a subject they subsequently don't like or help retain those who are already in a course. More directly, open textbooks provide a free resource, saving students or schools money on purchasing these. MOOCs and OERs themselves provide opportunities for the leisure learner to satisfy a learning need without any financial investment, although they may then desire to go further in to study.

These three areas of social relevance, graduate suitability and financial cost are all recurring themes for universities. Openness is not the only solution to them, but it is one that is relatively easy to adopt and could address them without resorting to the whole-sale revolution approach that is often called for.

The Price of Openness

In Chapter 1, the analogy with greenwashing was made, with openwashing demonstrating that the label 'open' has acquired a certain market value and is worth proclaiming. While I would resist a dogmatic approach to allowing the use of the term, what this suggests is that one response to the use of openness is not to allow the use of the term lightly. If 'openness' has a market value, then we should demand of those who use it for their benefit some adherence to general principles of openness – for example, that their content is openly licensed.

One such example that is often encountered is the number of research articles that address open education in some form but which aren't published under an open access licence. It is ironic to say the least to encounter an article about the benefits of OERs and be asked to pay US\$40 to access it.

As was outlined in Chapter 3, increasingly there is a shift to make all articles open access anyway, but for any research in the field of open education (MOOCs, OA, OER, open data, etc.), it is reasonable to expect that the resultant publications are open access. As soon as a researcher commences in this area they are,

I would argue, morally obliged to publish their results under an open access agreement, whether it is Green or Gold route. This research is only possible because others have been open (even if they are critical of it), so the researcher is therefore beholden to reciprocate in a like manner. Openness is the route that facilitates this research and it also has value; people will want to read the article because it is about openness. Both the researchers and the publishers are benefitting from openness and shouldn't get these benefits for free – open access is the price of admission.

Similar examples may be found with MOOCs or technology platforms. If the 'open' moniker is adopted, then it comes with at least a challenge as to the extent of that openness.

The Open Virus

One way of viewing the open approach is analogous to a virus. Once adopted, it tends to spread across many other aspects. For example, in personal practice, once an academic publishes a paper under an open access license, then there is then an incentive to use various forms of social media to promote that paper, which as we saw in Chapter 7, can positively impact views and citations. Similarly, although the free cost is the initial driving factor for the adoption of open textbooks, once this has become established, the ability to adapt the material to better suit their particular needs becomes an important factor for educators. When educators and institutions begin to use OERs in their own teaching material, then the question arises as to why they are not then reciprocating. As we saw in Chapter 4, this practice is not guaranteed and may be slow to penetrate, but the act of sharing becomes legitimised by the adoption of materials from high-reputation institutions.

It is no coincidence that many of the MOOC pioneers had also been early adopters of open access, active bloggers and advocates of open licenses. Creating open courses seemed the next logical step, because they were interested in the possibilities that openness offered and had seen the benefits elsewhere in their practice. This spread of the open virus is by no means guaranteed; many practitioners remain immune, and for others the open practice remains limited to a very specific function. But it does seem to be a pattern that is repeated across all aspects of open practice. It is significant in the context of this book, because if we are now entering a transition period when open practice enters the mainstream, then (to stretch the metaphor) the number of people 'exposed' to the open virus increases dramatically and it becomes a pandemic. It is also significant because it requires individuals to be the agents of action. The compartmentalising of openness into specific projects or outsourcing it to external providers creates a form of barrier that isolates individual educators from exposure. The impact of openness is thus contained. One might conclude, from the virus metaphor, that a good approach to spread open practice is to seek easy entry points or Trojan horses, where the initial aspect of openness can be seeded. However, as with the LMS example, this initial easy success should not become the endpoint.

Conclusions

In this chapter, a number of aspects of openness have been considered which have implications for its future direction. Policy will be the lever by which open practice can become sustainable and mainstream. However, the LMS lesson demonstrates that any such policy approaches must also allow sufficient scope for innovation and experimentation, as these are the route to the real benefits of openness. The innovation that openness affords provides solutions to a number of the very substantial challenges facing higher education. In some respects the digital, open revolution is the cause of these challenges, and it is also the solution. This victory of openness is evidenced by the value that the term 'open' acquires as a marketing phrase, and one response to this is to make demands on those who seek to bend the term to their own ends. Lastly, it was suggested that openness has a virus-like ability to spread across many different practices once it has been adopted in one place.

What all of these directions for openness have in common is ownership. In this book I have attempted to establish two arguments about openness: that it is a successful approach to adopt for much of education and that it is now at a crucial stage regarding its future direction. Underlying the success of openness for education is the opportunity for experimentation and innovation. MOOCs, OERs, open access and open scholarship have all been the result of those working within higher education seeking to engage with the possibilities that openness allows. Having won the first battle – that it is an effective way to operate – it is essential that the second battle regarding the future direction of openness is not lost by abdicating responsibility and ownership. This is not to say that only universities can engage with open education; there are many different ways it can be approached, and it would be foolish to be prescriptive. But it does mean that those working in education need to engage with the debates set out in this book and decide best how openness can work for them. Failure to do so will mean that others decide this on their behalf.

Bibliography

Aaronovitch, D. (2013) 'Even if everything's free, there can be a price: The death of hacker Aaron Swartz reveals a young generation unaware of its own great power–or responsibilities'. *The Times*. January 17, 2013 p. 23.

Academia.edu (2103) 'Traction'. http://www.academia.edu/hiring/traction. [Last accessed 7th September 2014]

Allen, N. (2013). 'Affordable Textbooks for Washington Students: An Updated Cost Analysis of the Open Course Library'. *Student Public Interest Research Groups*. http://www.studentpirgs.org/sites/student/files/resources/PIRG%20OCL.pdf. [Last accessed 7th September 2014]

Anderson K. (2012) 'Does Open Access Tackle, Perpetuate, or Exacerbate the Matthew Effect?' *The Scholarly Kitchen*. http://scholarlykitchen.sspnet.org/2012/10/04/does-open-access-tackle-perpetuate-or-exacerbate-the-matthew-effect/. [Last accessed 7th September 2014]

Bacsich P. (2013) *POERUP – Policy advice for universities (release 1)*. http://www.scribd.com/doc/169430544/Policies-at-EU-level-for-OER-uptake-in-universities. [Last accessed 7th September 2014]

Banyai M. and Glover, T. (2012) 'Evaluating Research Methods on Travel Blogs'. *Journal of Travel Research* 51: 267–277.

Barber, M., Donnelly, K. and Rizv, S. (2103) 'An avalanche is coming: Higher education and the revolution ahead'. *The Institute of Public Policy Research.* http://www.ippr.org/images/media/files/publication/2013/03/avalanche-is-coming_Mar2013_10432.pdf. [Last accessed 7th September 2014]

Bates, T. (1995) *Technology, Open Learning and Distance Education.* London: Routledge.

Bates, T. (2014) 'Time to retire from online learning?' http://www.tonybates.ca/2014/04/15/time-to-retire-from-online-learning/. [Last accessed 7th September 2014]

Beall, J. (2010) 'Predatory Open-Access Scholarly Publishers'. *The Charleston Advisor*, 11, n. 4, pp. 10–17.

Becher, T. (1994) 'The significance of disciplinary differences'. *Studies in Higher Education*, 19(2), p. 151.

Bell, S. and Lane, A. (1998) 'From Teaching to Learning: Technological Potential and Sustainable, Supported Open Learning'. *Systemic Practice and Action Research,* Vol. 11, No. 6, pp. 629–650.

Biemiller L (2014) 'Open Course Library Sees Little Use in Washington's Community Colleges'. *The Chronicle of Higher Education.* January 31, 2014. http://chronicle.com/blogs/wiredcampus/open-course-library-sees-little-use-in-washingtons-community-colleges/50017. [Last accessed 7th September 2014]

Blackenhorn, D. (2012) 'MOOCs: End of higher ed as we know it?' *MSN Money.* http://money.msn.com/technology-investment/post.aspx?post=14a3a055-bae6-4245-8280-702689db938b. [Last accessed 7th September 2014]

Bohannon, J. (2013) 'Who's Afraid of Peer Review?' *Science* 4, October 2013: 342 (6154), 60–65. doi:10.1126/science.342.6154.60.

Bonstein, J. (2009) 'Homesick for a Dictatorship: Majority of Eastern Germans Feel Life Better under Communism'. *Spiegel*

Online, July 3, 2009. http://www.spiegel.de/international/germany/homesick-for-a-dictatorship-majority-of-eastern-germans-feel-life-better-under-communism-a-634122.html [Last accessed 7th September 2014]

Booker, E. (2013) 'Will MOOCs Massively Disrupt Higher Education?' *Information Week.* August 30, 2013 http://www.informationweek.com/software/will-moocs-massively-disrupt-higher-education/d/d-id/1111357. [Last accessed 7th September 2014]

Bossu, C., Bull, B. and Brown, M. (2012) 'Opening up Down Under: the role of open educational resources in promoting social inclusion in Australia'. *Distance Education* Vol. 33, Iss. 2, 2012.

Boston Consulting Group. (2012) 'The Open Education Resources ecosystem: An evaluation of the OER movement's current state and its progress toward mainstream adoption'. http://www.hewlett.org/sites/default/files/The%20Open%20Educational%20Resources%20Ecosystem_1.pdf. [Last accessed 7th September 2014]

Boyle, J. (2008) 'Obama's team must fight "cultural agoraphobia"', *Financial Times*, December 17, 2008.

Brennan, J., King, R. and Lebeau, Y. (2004) 'The Role of Universities in the Transformation of Societies'. *Centre for Higher Education Research and Information.* http://www.open.ac.uk/cheri/documents/transf-final-report.pdf. [Last accessed 7th September 2014]

Buchanan, R. (2013) 'University degrees are worth over £100,000 in additional earnings'. *The Independent,* June 27, 2013. http://www.independent.co.uk/student/news/university-degrees-are-worth-over-100000-in-additional-earnings-8676251.html. [Last accessed 7th September 2014]

Budapest Open Access Initiative. (2002) 'Read the Budapest Open Access Initiative'. http://www.budapestopenaccessinitiative.org/read. [Last accessed 7th September 2014]

Campbell, G. (2012). Open Ed 12 – Gardner Campbell Keynote – Ecologies of Yearning. http://www.youtube.com/watch?v=kIzA4ItynYw. [Last accessed 7th September 2014]

Canetti, E. (1962) *Crowds and power*. Macmillan.

Caplan-Bricker, N. (2013) 'This North Carolina Campus Was Meant to Show Off the Future of Online Education. It hasn't gone according to plan'. *New Republic,* December 22, 2013 http://www.newrepublic.com/article/116014/black-mountain-sole-mooc-campus-online-learners-has-rough-start. [Last accessed 7th September 2014]

Carr, D. F. (2013) 'Udacity CEO Says MOOC "Magic Formula" Emerging'. *Information Week,* August 19, 2013. http://www.informationweek.com/software/udacity-ceo-says-mooc-magic-formula-emerging/d/d-id/1111221. [Last accessed 7th September 2014]

Caulfield, M. (2013) 'As we were saying… (Coursera as Provider of Courseware)'. http://hapgood.us/2013/05/30/as-we-were-saying-coursera-as-provider-of-courseware/. [Last accessed 7th September 2014]

Chafkin, M. (2013) 'Udacity's Sebastian Thrun, godfather of free online education, changes course'. *Fast Company,* November 14, 2013. http://www.fastcompany.com/3021473/udacity-sebastian-thrun-uphill-climb. [Last accessed 7th September 2014]

Cheverie, J. F., Boettcher, J. and Buschman, J. (2009) 'Digital Scholarship in the University Tenure and Promotion Process: A Report on the Sixth Scholarly Communication Symposium at Georgetown University Library'. *Journal of Scholarly Publishing* 40.3 (2009): 219–230 http://muse.jhu.edu/journals/journal_of_scholarly_publishing/summary/v040/40.3.cheverie.html. [Last accessed 7th September 2014]

Christensen, C. M. (1997) *The innovator's dilemma: when new technologies cause great firms to fail*. Boston: Harvard Business School Press.

Christensen, C. M., Horn, M. B. and Johnson, C. W. (2008) *Disrupting class: how disruptive innovation will change the way the world learns*. New York: McGraw-Hill.

Christensen, C.M., Horn, M. and Staker, H. (2013) 'Is K–12 Blended Learning Disruptive? An introduction of the theory of hybrids'. *The Christensen Institute.* http://www.christenseninstitute.

org/wp-content/uploads/2013/05/Is-K-12-Blended-Learning-Disruptive.pdf. [Last accessed 7th September 2014]

Christensen, G., Steinmetz, A., Alcorn, B., Bennett, A., Woods, D. and Emanuel, E. (2013) 'The MOOC Phenomenon: Who Takes Massive Open Online Courses and Why?' *SSRN*. http://papers.ssrn.com/sol3/papers.cfm?abstract_id=2350964. [Last accessed 7th September 2014]

Clark, D. (2013) 'MOOCs: more action in 1 year than last 1000 years'. http://donaldclarkplanb.blogspot.co.uk/2013/04/moocs-more-action-in-1-year-than-last.html. [Last accessed 7th September 2014]

Clarke, R. (2007). 'The cost profiles of alternative approaches to journal publishing'. *First Monday*, 12(12). doi:10.5210/fm.v12i12.2048.

Cormier, D. (2008) 'Open Educational Resources: The implications for educational development (SEDA)'. http://davecormier.com/edblog/2009/11/24/open-educational-resources-the-implications-for-educational-development-seda/. [Last accessed 7th September 2014]

Cormier, D. (2013) 'What do you mean... open?' http://davecormier.com/edblog/2013/04/12/what-do-you-mean-open/. [Last accessed 7th September 2014]

The Cost of Knowledge. (2012) http://thecostofknowledge.com/. [Last accessed 7th September 2014]

Costa, C. (2013) 'The participatory web in the context of academic research: Landscapes of change and conflicts'. *PhD thesis*, University of Salford.

Coughlan, T. (2013) 'Harvard plans to boldly go with "Spocs"'. *BBC News* September 24, 2013 http://www.bbc.co.uk/news/business-24166247. [Last accessed 7th September 2014]

Coursera. (2013a) 'Our Student Numbers (as of September 14, 2013)'. https://www.coursera.org/about/community. [Last accessed 7th September 2014]

Coursera. (2013b) 'Introducing Signature Track'. Coursera blog http://blog.coursera.org/post/40080531667/signaturetrack. [Last accessed 7th September 2014]

Coursera. (2013c) '10 US State University Systems and Public Institutions Join Coursera to Explore MOOC-based Learning and Collaboration on Campus'. Coursera Blog http://blog.coursera.org/post/51696469860/10-us-state-university-systems-and-public-institutions. [Last accessed 7th September 2014]

Creative Commons. (2013a) 'What is OER?' http://wiki.creativecommons.org/What_is_OER%3F. [Last accessed 7th September 2014]

Creative Commons. (2013b) OER Policy Registry http://wiki.creativecommons.org/OER_Policy_Registry. [Last accessed 7th September 2014]

Dahlstrom, E., Walker, J. D. and Dziuban, C. (2013) *ECAR Study of Undergraduate Students and Information Technology, 2013* (Research Report). Louisville, CO: EDUCAUSE Center for Analysis and Research, September 2013 http://www.educause.edu/library/resources/ecar-study-undergraduate-students-and-information-technology-2013. [Last accessed 7th September 2014]

Daly, U., Glapa-Grossklag, J., Gaudet, D. and Illowsky, B. (2013) 'Discover How OER Adoption Fosters Policy and Practice Changes at Community Colleges'. *OCWC Conference 2013*. http://presentations.ocwconsortium.org/ind2013_discover_how_oer_adoption_fosters_policy/. [Last accessed 7th September 2014]

Daniel, J. S. (2012) 'Making Sense of MOOCs: Musings in a Maze of Myth, Paradox and Possibility'. *JIME* http://jime.open.ac.uk/jime/article/view/2012-18. [Last accessed 7th September 2014]

Davis, P. M. (2011) 'Open access, readership, citations: a randomized controlled trial of scientific journal publishing'. *The FASEB Journal*, *25*(7), 2129–2134.

Davis, P. M., Lewenstein, B., Simon, D., Booth, J. and Connolly, M. (2008) 'Open access publishing, article downloads, and citations: randomised controlled trial'. *BMJ*, 337:a568, July 31, 2008 http://www.bmj.com/content/337/bmj.a568. [Last accessed 8th September 2014]

De Los Arcos, B. (2014) 'Flipped Learning and OER: Survey Results'. http://oscailte.wordpress.com/2014/03/13/research-findings-on-flipped-learning-and-oer/. [Last accessed 8th September 2014]

Debarbieux, B. and Rudaz G. (2008) 'Linking mountain identities throughout the world: the experience of Swiss communities'. *Cultural Geographies* 15: 497–517.

DeJong, R. (2013) 'What Do MOOCs Cost? Minding the Campus'. http://www.mindingthecampus.com/2013/09/what_do_moocs_cost/. [Last accessed 8th September 2014]

Delmas, M. A. and Burbano, V. (2011) 'The Drivers of Greenwashing' *California Management Review*, 54(1), 64–87.

Dennen, V. P. (2009) 'Constructing academic alter-egos: identity issues in a blog-based community'. *Identity in the Information Society*, 2(1), 23–38.

Downes, S. (2001). 'Learning Objects: Resources for Distance Education Worldwide'. *The International Review of Research in Open and Distance Learning*, 2(1). http://www.irrodl.org/index.php/irrodl/article/view/32/378. [Last accessed 8th September 2014]

Downes, S. (2014) 'Like Reading a Newspaper' http://halfanhour.blogspot.co.uk/2014/03/like-reading-newspaper.html. [Last accessed 8th September 2014]

Dvorak, J. (2004) 'The Myth of Disruptive Technology'. *PC Mag.*, August 17, 2004 http://www.pcmag.com/article2/0,2817,1628049,00.asp. [Last accessed 8th September 2014]

Edwards, R. and Shulenburger, D. (2002) 'The High Cost of Scholarly Journals (And What to Do About It)'. *Change*, vol. 35, Issue 6, p. 10.

Esposito, A. (2013) 'Neither digital or open. Just researchers: Views on digital/open scholarship practices in an Italian university'. *First Monday*, 18(1). doi:10.5210/fm.v18i1.3881.

ESRC. (2010) 'Success rates'. http://www.esrc.ac.uk/about-esrc/mission-strategy-priorities/demand-management/success-rates.aspx. [Last accessed 8th September 2014]

Etzkowitz, H., Webster, A., Gebhardt, C. and Terra, B. R. C. (2000) 'The future of the university and the university of the future: evolution of ivory tower to entrepreneurial paradigm'. *Research policy*, 29(2), 313–330.

Ewins, R. (2005) 'Who are You? Weblogs and Academic Identity'. *E–Learning*, 2:4.

Farrow, R. and Frank-Bristow, S. (2014) 'A grand tour of OER policy'. *OER 14*, Newcastle, April 28–29, 2014 http://www.medev.ac.uk/oer14/62/view/. [Last accessed 8th September 2014]

Fazackerley, A. (2012) 'UK universities are wary of getting on board the MOOC train'. *The Guardian,* December 3, 2012 http://www.guardian.co.uk/education/2012/dec/03/massive-online-open-courses-universities. [Last accessed 8th September 2014]

Feldstein, A., Martin, M., Hudson, A., Warren, K., Hilton III, J. and Wiley, D. (2013) 'Open Textbooks and Increased Student Outcomes'. *European Journal of Open, Distance and E-Learning* http://www.eurodl.org/index.php?p=archives&year=2012&halfyear=2&article=533. [Last accessed 8th September 2014]

Finch Group. (2012) 'Accessibility, sustainability, excellence: how to expand access to research publications.' Research Information Network. http://www.researchinfonet.org/publish/finch/. [Last accessed 8th September 2014]

Finley, K. (2011) 'How to Spot Openwashing'. *ReadWrite.Com* http://readwrite.com/2011/02/03/how_to_spot_openwashing. [Last accessed 8th September 2014]

Fransman, J., Couglan, T., Farrow, R. and Weller, M. (2012) 'Digital Scholarship at the OU: Twitter practices in the arts and science faculties'. Open University Report http://nogoodreason.typepad.co.uk/Digital%20Scholarship%20Project%20Report%20DRAFT%201.doc. [Last accessed 8th September 2014]

Friedman, T. L. (2013) 'Revolution Hits the Universities'. *New York Times,* Jan 26, 2013 http://www.nytimes.com/2013/01/27/opinion/sunday/friedman-revolution-hits-the-universities.html?_r=0. [Last accessed 8th September 2014]

Fulton, K. (2012) 'Inside the Flipped Classroom'. *T.H.E. Journal Digital Edition*, November 2012 [online]. http://the-journal.com/Articles/2012/04/11/The-flipped-classroom.aspx?Page=1. [Last accessed 8th September 2014]

Gargouri, Y., Hajjem, C., Larivière, V., Gingras, Y., Carr, L., et al. (2010) 'Self-Selected or Mandated, Open Access Increases Citation Impact for Higher Quality Research'. *PLoS ONE* 5(10): e13636. doi:10.1371/journal.pone.0013636.

Geere, D. (2011) 'The history of Creative Commons'. *Wired*, December 13, 2011 http://www.wired.co.uk/news/archive/2011-12/13/history-of-creative-commons. [Last accessed 8th September 2014]

Geist, M. (2006) 'Patent battle over teaching tools'. *BBC News*, August 14, 2006 http://news.bbc.co.uk/1/hi/technology/4790485.stm. [Last accessed 8th September 2014]

Gilmore, D. (2012) 'B.C. to lead Canada in offering students free, open textbooks'. BC Columbia Press release 2012AEIT0010-001581 http://www2.news.gov.bc.ca/news_releases_2009-2013/2012AEIT0010-001581.htm. [Last accessed 8th September 2014]

Givler, P. (2002) 'University Press Publishing in the United States'. *Scholarly Publishing: Books, Journals, Publishers and Libraries in the Twentieth Century*, edited by Richard E. Abel and Lyman W. Newman, Wiley.

Goldstein, B. (2013) 'As MOOCs Move Mainstream Universities Must Pay to Play'. *Huffington Post* http://www.huffingtonpost.com/buck-goldstein/as-moocs-move-mainstream-_b_4170524.html. [Last accessed 8th September 2014]

Golle, P. (2006) 'Revisiting the uniqueness of simple demographics in the US population'. *Proceedings of the 5th ACM workshop on Privacy in electronic society*, ACM. pp. 77–80.

Government Accounts Office. (2005) 'College Textbooks: Enhanced Offerings Appear to Drive Recent Price Increases' http://www.gao.gov/assets/250/247332.pdf. [Last accessed 8th September 2014]

Greco, A. and Wharton, R. (2010) 'The Market Demand for University Press Books 2008–15'. *Journal of Scholarly Publishing*, 42(1), 1–15.

Green, C. (2013) 'The Impact of Open Textbooks at OpenStax College'. http://creativecommons.org/weblog/entry/38890. [Last accessed 8th September 2014]

Groom, J. (2011) 'ds106: We're open and you're invited' http://bavatuesdays.com/ds106-were-open-and-youre-invited/. [Last accessed 8th September 2014]

Groom, J. (2014) 'Innovation lost' http://bavatuesdays.com/innovation-lost/. [Last accessed 8th September 2014]

Groom, J. and Lamb, B. (2014) 'Reclaiming Innovation'. *EDUCAUSE Review*, May/June 2014, vol. 49, no. 3.

Gruzd, A., Staves, K. and Wilk, A. (2011) 'Tenure and promotion in the age of online social media'. *Proc. Am. Soc. Info. Sci. Tech.*, 48: 1–9. doi: 10.1002/meet.2011.14504801154.

Hajjem, C., Harnad, S. and Gingras, Y. (2005) 'Ten-Year Cross-Disciplinary Comparison of the Growth of Open Access and How it Increases Research Citation Impact'. *IEEE Data Eng. Bull*, December 2005, vol. 28, No. 4 http://sites.computer.org/debull/A05dec/hajjem.pdf. [Last accessed 8th September 2014]

Haklev, S. (2010) 'The Chinese national top level courses project: Using open educational resources to promote quality in undergraduate teaching'. *PhD Thesis*, University of Toronto http://reganmian.net/top-level-courses/Haklev_Stian_201009_MA_thesis.pdf. [Last accessed 8th September 2014]

Hall, R. (2013) 'MOOCs and Neo-liberalism: for a critical response' http://www.richard-hall.org/2013/07/11/moocs-and-neoliberalism-for-a-critical-response/. [Last accessed 8th September 2014]

Harnad, S. (2012) 'Why the UK Should Not Heed the Finch Report'. *LSE Impact Blog* http://blogs.lse.ac.uk/impactofsocialsciences/2012/07/04/why-the-uk- should-not-heed-the-finch-report/. [Last accessed 8th September 2014]

Hemmings, B. C., Rushbrook, P. and Smith, E. (2007) 'Academics' Views on Publishing Refereed Works: A Content Analysis'. *Higher Education*, (2), 307. doi:10.2307/29735112.

William and Flora Hewlett Foundation. (n.d.) 'Open Educational Resources' http://www.hewlett.org/programs/education/open-educational-resources. [Last accessed 8th September 2014]

William and Flora Hewlett Foundation. (2013) 'White Paper: Open Educational Resources – Breaking the Lockbox on Education' http://www.hewlett.org/library/hewlett-foundation-publication/white-paper-open-educational-resources. [Last accessed 8th September 2014]

Henkel, M. (2005) 'Academic identity and autonomy in a changing policy environment'. *Higher Education* 49: 155–176.

Heussner, K. M. (2013) 'Coursera hits $1M in revenue through verified certificates'. *GigaOm* http://gigaom.com/2013/09/12/coursera-hits-1m-in-revenue-through-verified-certificates/. [Last accessed 8th September 2014]

High, P. (2013) 'Udacity CEO Sebastian Thrun on the Future of Education' *Forbes*, September 12, 2013 http://www.forbes.com/sites/peterhigh/2013/12/09/udacity-ceo-sebastian-thrun-on-the-future-of-education/. [Last accessed 8th September 2014]

High, P. (2014) 'Salman Khan, The Most Influential Person in Education Technology'. *Forbes*, Jan 6, 2014 http://www.forbes.com/sites/peterhigh/2014/01/06/salman-khan-the-most-influential-person-in-education-technology/. [Last accessed 8th September 2014]

Higher education statistics agency. (2013) Students & qualifiers. http://www.hesa.ac.uk/content/view/1897/239/. [Last accessed 8th September 2014]

Hill, P. (2013) 'The Most Thorough Summary (to date) of MOOC Completion Rates' http://mfeldstein.com/the-most-thorough-summary-to-date-of-mooc-completion-rates/. [Last accessed 8th September 2014]

Hirst, T. (2012) 'Socially Positioning #Sherlock and Dr John Watson's Blog…' http://blog.ouseful.info/2012/01/08/socially-positioning-sherlock/. [Last accessed 8th September 2014]

Hirst, T. (2013) 'What Role, If Any, Does Spending Data Have to Play in Local Council Budget Consultations?' http://blog.ouseful.info/2013/11/03/what-role-if-any-does-spending-data-have-to-play-in-local-council-budget-consultations/. [Last accessed 8th September 2014]

Holdren, J. (2013) Increasing Access to the Results of Federally Funded Scientific Research. *Office of Science and Technology*

*Policy*http://www.whitehouse.gov/sites/default/files/microsites/ostp/ostp_public_access_memo_2013.pdf [Last accessed 8th September 2014]

Holling, C. S. (1973) 'Resilience and stability of ecological systems'. *Annual Review Ecology Systems* 4: 1–23.

Hopkins, R. (2009) 'Resilience Thinking'. *Resurgence* 257.

Howard, J. (2012) 'Flat World Knowledge to Drop Free Access to Textbooks'. *The Chronicle of Higher Education* http://chronicle.com/blogs/wiredcampus/flat-world-knowledge-to-drop-free-access-to-textbooks/40780. [Last accessed 8th September 2014]

Idea. (2012) 'Higher-ed courses with massive enrollments: A revolution starts'. *Idea.org* http://www.idea.org/blog/2012/01/31/higher-ed-courses-with-massive-enrollments-a-revolution-starts/. [Last accessed 8th September 2014]

Jones, C., Aoki, K.; Rusman, E. and Schlusmans, K. (2009). 'A comparison of three Open Universities and their acceptance of Internet Technologies'. *Proceedings of the 23rd ICDE World Conference on Open Learning and Distance Education*, June 7–10, 2009, Maastricht, Netherlands

Jordan, K. (2013) 'Synthesising MOOC completion rates' http://moocmoocher.wordpress.com/2013/02/13/synthesising-mooc-completion-rates/. [Last accessed 8th September 2014]

Jordan, K. and Weller, M. (2013a) 'Design Responses to MOOC Completion Rates' http://nogoodreason.typepad.co.uk/no_good_reason/2013/12/design-responses-to-mooc-completion-rates.html. [Last accessed 8th September 2014]

Jordan, K. and Weller, M. (2013b) 'Redefining MOOC Completion Rates' http://nogoodreason.typepad.co.uk/no_good_reason/2013/12/redefining-mooc-completion-rates.html. [Last accessed 8th September 2014]

Kamenetz, A. (2010) *DIY U edupunks, edupreneurs, and the coming transformation of higher education,* Chelsea Green Publishing.

Kamenetz, A. (2012) 'How Coursera, a free online education service, will school us all'. *Fast Company,* September 2012 http://www.fastcompany.com/3000042/how-coursera-free-online-education-service-will-school-us-all. [Last accessed 8th September 2014]

Kane, M. (2012) 'Professional adventure tourists: Producing and selling stories of "authentic" identity'. *Tourist Studies*, December 2012, vol. 12, no. 3, pp. 268–286.

Kelty, C. M. (2008) *Two Bits. The Cultural Significance of Free Software*. Duke University.

Kernohan, D. (2013) 'Education is broken, somebody should do something' http://followersoftheapocalyp.se/education_is_broken/#sthash.GonQND8j.dpuf. [Last accessed 8th September 2014]

Khan Academy. (2013) 'Root Access: How to Scale your Startup to Millions of Users' http://www.youtube.com/watch?v=r7hC0oVPTVs. [Last accessed 8th September 2014]

Khan, S. and Noer, M. (2011) 'The History of Education' http://www.youtube.com/watch?v=LqTwDDTjb6g. [Last accessed 8th September 2014]

Kim, J. (2011) 'Pearson's OpenClass Free LMS: 4 Initial Challenges'. *Inside Higher Ed*, October 13, 2011 http://www.insidehighered.com/blogs/technology_and_learning/pearson_s_openclass_free_lms_4_initial_challenges. [Last accessed 8th September 2014]

Kizilcec, R. F., Piech, C., and Schneider, E. (2013) 'Deconstructing disengagement: analyzing learner subpopulations in massive open online courses'. *Proceedings of the Third International Conference on Learning Analytics and Knowledge*, ACM, pp. 170–179.

Knowledge Unlatched. (n.d.) 'How it works' http://www.knowledgeunlatched.org/about/how-it-works/. [Last accessed 8th September 2014]

Koller, D. (2012) 'What we're learning from online education'. *TED*, http://www.ted.com/talks/daphne_koller_what_we_re_learning_from_online_education. [Last accessed 8th September 2014]

Kolowich, S. (2013a) 'Coursera Snags $43-Million in Venture Capital'. *The Chronicle of Higher Education* http://chronicle.

com/blogs/wiredcampus/mooc-company-snags-43-million-in-venture-capital/44667. [Last accessed 8th September 2014]

Kolowich, S. (2013b) 'MOOCs Are Largely Reaching Privileged Learners, Survey Finds'. *Chronicle of Higher Education*, November 20, 2013. http://chronicle.com/blogs/wiredcampus/moocs-are-reaching-only-privileged-learners-survey-finds/48567. [Last accessed 8th September 2014]

Kolowich, S. (2013c) 'Georgia Tech and Coursera Try to Recover From MOOC Stumble'. *The Chronicle of Higher Education*, February 4, 2013 http://chronicle.com/blogs/wiredcampus/georgia-tech-and-coursera-try-to-recover-from-mooc-stumble/42167. [Last accessed 8th September 2014]

Kolowich, S. (2013d) 'edX Drops Plans to Connect MOOC Students with Employers'. *The Chronicle of Higher Education*, December 16, 2013 http://chronicle.com/blogs/wiredcampus/edx-drops-plans-to-connect-mooc-students-with-employers/48987. [Last accessed 8th September 2014]

Kolowich, S. (2013e) 'Faculty Backlash Grows Against Online Partnerships'. *The Chronicle of Higher Education,* May 6, 2013 http://chronicle.com/article/Faculty-Backlash-Grows-Against/139049/. [Last accessed 8th September 2014]

Kop, R. (2011) 'The challenges to connectivist learning on open online networks: Learning experiences during a massive open online course'. *The International Review of Research in Open and Distance Learning,* North America, 12, Jan. 2011. http://www.irrodl.org/index.php/irrodl/article/view/882/1689. [Last accessed 8th September 2014]

Kortemeyer, G. (2013) 'Ten Years Later: Why Open Educational Resources Have Not Noticeably Affected Higher Education, and Why We Should Care'. *Educause Review,* Nov/Dec 2013 http://www.educause.edu/ero/article/ten-years-later-why-open-educational-resources-have-not-noticeably-affected-higher-education-and-why-we-should-ca. [Last accessed 8th September 2014]

Laakso, M., Welling, P., Bukvova, H., Nyman, L., Björk, B-C., et al. (2011) 'The Development of Open Access Journal Publishing from 1993 to 2009'. *PLoS ONE* 6(6): e20961. doi: 10.1371/journal.pone.0020961.

Lane, A. (2009) 'The Impact of Openness on Bridging Educational Digital Divides'. *The International Review of Research in Open and Distance Learning*, vol. 10, no. 5 http://www.irrodl.org/index.php/irrodl/article/view/637. [Last accessed 8th September 2014]

Lane, A. (2012) 'A review of the role of national policy and institutional mission in European distance teaching universities with respect to widening participation in higher education study through open educational resources'. *Distance Education*, 33(2) pp. 135–150.

Laurillard, D. (2014) 'Five myths about MOOCs'. *The Times Higher Education,* Jan 16, 2014 http://www.timeshighereducation.co.uk/comment/opinion/five-myths-about-moocs/2010480.article. [Last accessed 8th September 2014]

Lawrence, S. (2001) 'Free online availability substantially increases a paper's impact'. *Nature*, May 31, 2001 http://www.nature.com/nature/debates/e-access/Articles/lawrence.html. [Last accessed 8th September 2014]

Leckart, S. (2012) 'The Stanford Education Experiment Could Change Higher Learning Forever'. *Wired* http://www.wired.com/wiredscience/2012/03/ff_aiclass/. [Last accessed 8th September 2014]

Lessig, L. (2010) 'Sorkin vs. Zuckerberg'. *The New Republic,* October 1, 2010 http://www.newrepublic.com/article/books-and-arts/78081/sorkin-zuckerberg-the-social-network?page=0,1. [Last accessed 8th September 2014]

Levy, A. (2013) 'Graduates lack basic skills and are more interested in "what a job can do for them, not what they have to offer an employer"'. *Daily Mail*, March 16, 2013 http://www.dailymail.co.uk/news/article-2294249/Graduates-lack-basic-skills-interested-job-offer-employer.html#ixzz30Z4kJjwf. [Last accessed 8th September 2014]

Lewin, T. (2013) 'After Setbacks, Online Courses Are Rethought'. *New York Times*, December 10, 2013 http://www.nytimes.

com/2013/12/11/us/after-setbacks-online-courses-are-rethought.html? [Last accessed 8th September 2014]

Liyanagunawardena, T., Williams, S. and Adams, A. (2013) 'The impact and reach of MOOCs: A developing countries' perspective'. *eLearning Papers* (33). ISSN 1887–1542.

Mason, R. (2000). 'From distance education to online education'. *The Internet and Higher Education*, 3(1-2) pp. 63–74.

McAndrew, P., Santos, A., Lane, A., Godwin, S., Okada, A., Wilson, T., Connolly, T., Ferreira, G., Buckingham Shum, S., Bretts, J. and Webb, R. (2009). *OpenLearn Research Report 2006–2008*, The Open University. Milton Keynes, England http://oro.open.ac.uk/17513/. [Last accessed 8th September 2014]

McGill, L. (2012) JISC OER Infokit https://openeducationalresources.pbworks.com/w/page/24836480/Home. [Last accessed 8th September 2014]

McGill, L., Falconer, I., Dempster, J.A., Littlejohn, A. and Beetham, H. (2013) 'Journeys to Open Educational Practice: UKOER/SCORE Review Final Report'. JISC https://oersynth.pbworks.com/w/page/60338879/HEFCE-OER-Review-Final-Report. [Last accessed 8th September 2014]

McGuigan, G. S. and Russell, R. D. (2008) 'The business of academic publishing: A strategic analysis of the academic journal publishing industry and its impact on the future of scholarly publishing'. *Electronic Journal of Academic and Special Librarianship*, 9(3). http://southernlibrarianship.icaap.org/content/v09n03/mcguigan_g01.html. [Last accessed 8th September 2014]

Mead, G. H. (1934) *Mind, Self, and Society. From the Standpoint of a Social Behaviorist*. Chicago: University of Chicago Press.

Metro. (2008) 'Pupil truancy hits all-time high' February 26 2008. http://metro.co.uk/2008/02/26/pupil-truancy-hits-all-time-high-10110/. [Last accessed 8th September 2014]

MOOC Research Group. (2013) *MOOCs @ Edinburgh 2013: Report #1* https://www.era.lib.ed.ac.uk/handle/1842/6683. [Last accessed 8th September 2014]

Morozov, E. (2013) 'The Meme Hustler'. *The Baffler* No. 22, 2013 http://www.thebaffler.com/past/the_meme_hustler.   [Last accessed 8th September 2014]

Newfield, C. (2013) 'Where Are the Savings?' *Inside Higher Ed,* June 24, 2013 http://www.insidehighered.com/views/2013/ 06/24/essay-sees-missing-savings-georgia-techs-much-discussed-mooc-based-program. [Last accessed 8th September 2014]

Noam, E. M. (1995) 'Electronics and the dim future of the university'. *Science* 270, 247–247.

Noble, D. F. (1998). 'Digital diploma mills: The automation of higher education'. *Science as culture*, 7(3), 355–368.

O'Reilly, T. (2005) 'What Is Web 2.0: Design Patterns and Business Models for the Next Generation of Software' http://oreilly. com/pub/a/web2/archive/what-is-web-20.html?page=1. [Last accessed 8th September 2014]

OCWC. (2013) User Feedback Survey http://www.ocwconsortium. org/projects/surveyresults/ [Last accessed 8th September 2014]

OECD. (2013) *Education at a Glance 2013,* OECD http://www. oecd.org /edu/eag.htm. [accessed November 2013]

OER Research Hub. (2013) http://oerresearchhub.org/. [Last accessed 8th September 2014]

OER Research Hub (2014) OER Impact Map http://oermap.org/. [Last accessed 8th September 2014]

Ohm, P. (2009) 'Broken Promises of Privacy: Responding to the Surprising Failure of Anonymization'. *UCLA Law Review*, vol. 57, p. 1701, 2010; U of Colorado Law Legal Studies Research Paper No. 9–12. Available at SSRN: http://ssrn.com/ abstract=1450006. [Last accessed 8th September 2014]

Open Citation Project. (2013) http://opcit.eprints.org/oacitation-biblio.html.

Open Knowledge Foundation. (n.d.) Our mission https://okfn. org/about/. [Last accessed 8th September 2014]

Open Knowledge Foundation. (n.d.) Open Definition http:// opendefinition.org/. [Last accessed 8th September 2014]

OpenStax. (2013) http://openstaxcollege.org/. [Last accessed 8th September 2014]

OpenStax Adapted modules: http://cnx.org/content/expanded_ browse_authors?author=OpenStaxCollege&subset= derivedfrom&sorton=popularity&cachekey=content/

expanded_browse_authors%3Fauthor%3DOpenStaxColle
ge%26subset%3Dderivedfrom%26letter%3DO%3Eforks&
letter=O&b_size=100&filename=Statistics_results&view_
mode=statistics&template=/content/expanded_browse_
authors. [Last accessed 8th September 2014]

OpenStax All current modules: http://cnx.org/content/expanded_
browse_authors?subset=by&sorton=popularity&cachekey=
content/expanded_browse_authors%3Fauthor%3DOpenStax
College%26subset%3Dderivedfrom%26letter%3DO%
3Eforks&letter=O&author=OpenStaxCollege&b_size=100&
filename=Statistics_results&view_mode=statistics&b_
start:int=1100&template=/content/expanded_browse_authors.
[Last accessed 8th September 2014]

Open University. (2012) *Financial Statements for the year ended
31 July 2012.* http://www.ouworldwide.com/pdfs/freedom_
information/financial_statement_2012.pdf. [Last accessed 8th
September 2014]

Oregon State University. (2014) 'OSU open textbook initiative aims
to reduce student costs, enhance learning' http://oregonstate.
edu/ua/ncs/archives/2014/feb/osu-open-textbook-initiative-
aims-reduce-student-costs-enhance-learning. [Last accessed
8th September 2014]

Pappano, L. (2012) 'The Year of the MOOC'. *New York Times*,
Nov 2, 2012 http://www.nytimes.com/2012/11/04/education/
edlife/massive-open-online-courses-are-multiplying-at-a-
rapid-pace.html? [Last accessed 8th September 2014]

Parr, C. (2013) 'Embrace Moocs or face decline, warns v-c'. *Times
Higher Education*, May 17, 2013 http://www.timeshigheredu-
cation.co.uk/news/embrace-moocs-or-face-decline-warns-v-
c/2003919.article. [Last accessed 8th September 2014]

Paul, R. (2013) 'School Choice: Part of the Solution to Our
Broken Education System'. *The Huffington Post*, July 29, 2013
http://www.huffingtonpost.com/sen-rand-paul/school-
choice_b_3660408.html. [Last accessed 8th September
2014]

Perna, L., Ruby, A., Boruch, R. Wang, N., Scull, J., Evans, C. and
Ahmad, S. (2013) 'The Life Cycle of a Million MOOC Users'.

MOOC Research Initiative Conference, Dallas, December 2013 http://www.gse.upenn.edu/pdf/ahead/perna_ruby_boruch_moocs_dec2013.pdf. [Last accessed 8th September 2014]

Perryman, L-A., Law, P., Law, A. (2013) 'Developing sustainable business models for institutions' provision of open educational resources: Learning from OpenLearn users' motivations and experiences'. *Proceedings: The Open and Flexible Higher Education Conference, 2013*, Paris. http://www.eadtu.eu/images/stories/Docs/Conference_2013/eadtu%20annual%20conference%202013%20-%20proceedings.pdf. [Last accessed 8th September 2014]

Peter, S., and Deimann, M. (2013) 'On the role of openness in education: A historical reconstruction'. *Open Praxis, 5*(1), 7–14. (doi: 10.5944/openpraxis.5.1.23)

Peters, M. A., and Britez, R. G. (Eds.) (2008) *Open education and education for openness.* Sense Publishers.

Petroski, H. (2012) *To Forgive Design: Understanding Failure.* Harvard University Press.

Pitt, R., Ebrahimi, N., McAndrew, P., and Coughlan, T. (2013). 'Assessing OER impact across organisations and learners: experiences from the Bridge to Success project'. *Journal of Interactive Media in Education*, 0(0). Retrieved March 21, 2014 http://jime.open.ac.uk/jime/article/view/2013-17. [Last accessed 8th September 2014]

Plashing Vole. (2013) 'This Sunday: World Exclusive – Blogger Makes Tasteless Jokes' http://plashingvole.blogspot.co.uk/2013/10/this-sunday-world-exclusive-blogger.html. [Last accessed 8th September 2014]

Procter, R., Williams, R., and Stewart, J. (2010) 'If you build it, will they come? How researchers perceive and use web 2.0'. *Research Information Network.*

Protalinski, E. (2013) 'Coursera partners with 13 new institutions to pass 100 total, eclipses 5 million students and 500 courses too'. *The NextWeb,* October 24, 2013 http://thenextweb.com/insider/2013/10/24/coursera-partners-13-institutions-pass-100-total-sees-5-million-students-500-courses/#!ALMfi. [Last accessed 8th September 2014]

Raymond, E. S. (2002) 'The law is an ass'. *Open Democracy* http://www.opendemocracy.net/media-copyrightlaw/article_246.jsp. [Last accessed 8th September 2014]

Raymond, E. S. (2008) *The Cathedral & the Bazaar: Musings on linux and open source by an accidental revolutionary.* O'Reilly. http://www.catb.org/~esr/writings/cathedral-bazaar/cathedral-bazaar/index.html. [Last accessed 8th September 2014]

RCUK. (2006) Report of the Research Councils UK Efficiency and Effectiveness of Peer Review Project http://www.rcuk.ac.uk/documents/documents/rcukprreport.pdf   http://www.rcuk.ac.uk/RCUK-prod/assets/documents/documents/rcukprreport.pdf. [Last accessed 8th September 2014]

Reclaim Open. (2013) http://open.media.mit.edu/. [Last accessed 8th September 2014]

Reed Elsevier. (2012) Annual Reports and Financial Statements. Reed Elsevier.

Richards, B. (2012) Glamorgan on iTunes U http://www.brichards.co.uk/design-and-development/glamorgan-on-itunes-u. [Last accessed 8th September 2014]

Rivard, R. (2013) 'Coursera's Contractual Elitism'. *Inside Higher Ed,* March 22, 2013 http://www.insidehighered.com/news/2013/03/22/coursera-commits-admitting-only-elite-universities. [Last accessed 8th September 2014]

ROARMAP, University of Southampton, http://roarmap.eprints.org. [Last accessed August 2014]

Robertson, A. (2013) 'iTunes U sees one billion content downloads, 60 percent from outside US'. *The Verge* http://www.theverge.com/2013/2/28/4039456 /itunes-u-sees-one-billion-content-downloads-60-percent-international. [Last accessed 8th September 2014]

Sandel, M. (2012) *What Money Can't Buy: The Moral Limits of Markets.* Penguin.

Schmallegger, D. and Carson, D. (2008) 'Blogs in tourism: Changing approaches to information exchange'. *Journal of Vacation Marketing* 14: 99–110.

Schmitt, J. (2013) 'The MOOC Revolution: How to Earn an Elite MBA for Free'. *Poets and Quants* http://poetsandquants.

com/2013/12/17/the-mooc-revolution-how-to-earn-an-elite-mba-for-free/. [Last accessed 8th September 2014]

Science Europe. (2013) 'Principles for the Transition to Open Access to Research Publications' http://www.scienceeurope. org/uploads/PublicDocumentsAndSpeeches/SE_OA_Pos_ Statement.pdf. [Last accessed 8th September 2014]

Selwyn, N. (2010) 'The educational significance of social media – a critical perspective'. *Keynote debate at Ed-Media conference 2010*, Toronto, June 28 to July 2, 2010 http://www.scribd.com/ doc/33693537/The-educational-significance-of-social-media-a-critical-perspective. [Last accessed 8th September 2014]

Shapiro, J. (2013) 'Grab A Share of Education's $6 Trillion Marketplace'. *Forbes*, September 11, 2013. http://www.forbes.com/ sites/jordanshapiro/2013/09/11/grab-a-share-of-educations-6-trillion-marketplace/. [Last accessed 8th September 2014]

Sharples, M., McAndrew, P., Weller, M., Ferguson, R., FitzGerald, E., Hirst, T., Mor, Y., Gaved, M., and Whitelock, D. (2012) *Innovating Pedagogy 2012: Open University Innovation Report 1*. Milton Keynes: The Open University.

Shirky, C. (2012) 'Napster, Udacity, and the Academy' http:// www.shirky.com/weblog/2012/11/napster-udacity-and-the-academy/. [Last accessed 8th September 2014]

Shirky, C. (2013) 'Your Massively Open Offline College Is Broken'. The Awl, February 7, 2013 http://www.theawl.com/2013/02/ how-to-save-college. [Last accessed 8th September 2014]

Siemens, G. (2012) 'MOOCs are really a platform' http://www. elearnspace.org/blog/2012/07/25/moocs-are-really-a-platform/. [Last accessed 8th September 2014]

Siemens, G. (2013) 'The Failure of Udacity' http://www.elearns-pace.org/blog/2013/11/15/the-failure-of-udacity/. [Last accessed 8th September 2014]

Siemens, G. (2014) 'The attack on our higher education system — and why we should welcome it'. *TED* blog http://blog.ted.com/ 2014/01/31/the-attack-on-our-higher-education-system-and-why-we-should-welcome-it/. [Last accessed 8th September 2014]

Simonite, T. (2013) 'As Data Floods In, Massive Open Online Courses Evolve'. *MIT Technology Review* http://www.technologyreview.

com/news/515396/as-data-floods-in-massive-open-online-courses-evolve/. [Last accessed 8th September 2014]

Snow, D. (2001) *Collective identities and expressive forms.* Irvine: Center for the Study of Democracy, p. 3.

Solomon, D. J. and Björk, B.-C. (2012) 'A study of open access journals using article processing charges'. *J. Am. Soc. Inf. Sci.,* 63: 1485–1495. doi: 10.1002/asi.22673.

Springer. (2011) *General Overview and Financial Performance 2011.* Springer Science and Business Media http://static.springer.com/sgw/documents/1175537/application/pdf/Overview+2011.pdf. [Last accessed 8th September 2014]

Stacey, P. (2013) 'The Pedagogy Of MOOCs' http://edtechfrontier.com/2013/05/11/the-pedagogy-of-moocs/. [Last accessed 8th September 2014]

Stallman, R. (2012) 'Why Open Source misses the point of Free Software' http://www.gnu.org/philosophy/open-source-misses-the-point.html. [Last accessed 8th September 2014]

Stark, K. (2013) *Don't Go Back to School: A Handbook for Learning Anything.*

Staton, M. (2014) 'The Degree Is Doomed'. *Harvard Business Review,* January 8, 2014 http://blogs.hbr.org/2014/01/the-degree-is-doomed/. [Last accessed 8th September 2014]

Stevenson, J. (2013) 'Grant applications are hard work' http://all-geo.org/volcan01010/2013/07/grant-applications-are-hard-work-includes-latex-template/. [Last accessed 8th September 2014]

Stryker, S. and Serpe, R. T. (1982) 'Commitment, identity salience, and role behavior: Theory and research example'. *Personality, roles, and social behavior,* pp. 199–218, New York: Springer.

Sweeney, L. (2000) 'Uniqueness of Simple Demographics in the U.S. Population', *LIDAPWP4.* Carnegie Mellon University, Laboratory for International Data Privacy, Pittsburgh, PA, 2000.

Taleb, N. N. (2012) *Antifragile: How to Live in a World We Don't Understand.* Allen Lane.

Tauber, T. (2013) 'When Media Companies Try to Become Education Companies'. *The Atlantic*, September 16,2013 http://www.theatlantic.com/education/archive/2013/09/when-media-companies-try-to-become-education-companies/279708/. [Last accessed 8th September 2014]

Taylor, M. (2013a) Hiding your research behind a paywall is immoral *The Guardian*, January 17, 2013 http://www.theguardian.com/science/blog/2013/jan/17/open-access-publishing-science-paywall-immoral. [Last accessed 8th September 2014]

Taylor, M. (2013b) 'Elsevier Steps Up Its War on Access'. http://svpow.com/2013/12/17/elsevier-steps-up-its-war-on-access/. [Last accessed 8th September 2014]

Terra Choice. (2010) 'The Sins of Greenwashing: home and family edition'. *Underwriters Laboratories* http://sinsofgreenwashing.org/index35c6.pdf. [Last accessed 8th September 2014]

The Economist. (2012) 'Learning new lessons'. *The Economist*, December 22, 2012 http://www.economist.com/news/international/21568738-online-courses-are-transforming-higher-education-creating-new-opportunities-best. [Last accessed 8th September 2014]

The Economist. (2013) 'The attack of the MOOCs'. *The Economist*, July 20, 2013. http://www.economist.com/news/business/21582001-army-new-online-courses-scaring-wits-out-traditional-universities-can-they. [Last accessed 8th September 2014]

Thibodeau, P. H. and Boroditsky, L. (2011) 'Metaphors We Think With: The Role of Metaphor in Reasoning'. *PLoS ONE* 6(2): e16782. doi:10.1371/journal.pone.0016782.

Udell, J. (2012) 'A Domain of One's Own'. *Wired,* July 27, 2012 http://www.wired.com/2012/07/a-domain-of-ones-own/. [Last accessed 8th September 2014]

UK Cabinet Office. (2013) Open Data Charter, June 18, 2013 https://www.gov.uk/government/publications/open-data-charter. [Last accessed 8th September 2014]

Unger, R. and Warfel, T. (2011) 'Getting Guerrilla With It'. *UX Magazine*, Article no. 620, February 15, 2011 http://

uxmag.com/articles/getting-guerrilla-with-it. [Last accessed 8th September 2014]

Veletsianos, G. (2012) 'Higher Education Scholars' Participation and Practices on Twitter'. *Journal of Computer Assisted Learning*, 28(4), 336–349.

Veletsianos, G., & Kimmons, R. (2012) 'Assumptions and challenges of open scholarship'. *The International Review of Research in Open and Distance Learning*, 13(4), 166–189. http://www.irrodl.org/index.php/irrodl/article/view/1313/2304. [Last accessed 8th September 2014]

Wadhwa, T. (2013) 'Justine Sacco, Internet Justice, and the Dangers of a Righteous Mob'. *Forbes*, December 23, 2013 http://www.forbes.com/sites/tarunwadhwa/2013/12/23/justine-sacco-internet-justice-and-the-dangers-of-a-righteous-mob/. [Last accessed 8th September 2014]

Walker, B. and Salt, D. (2006) *Resilience thinking: sustaining ecosystems and people in a changing world*. Island Press.

Walker, B., Holling, C. S.,Carpenter, S. R., and Kinzig A. (2004) 'Resilience, adaptability and transformability in social–ecological systems'. *Ecology and Society* 9(2): 5 http://www.ecologyandsociety.org/vol9/iss2/art5. [Last accessed 8th September 2014]

Warne, V. (2013) 'Mind the gap: 2013 Wiley survey reveals generational differences in authors' open access views and experience' http://exchanges.wiley.com/blog/2013/10/08/mind-the-gap-2013-wiley-open-access-survey/. [Last accessed 8th September 2014]

Watters, A. (2011) 'Pearson's "Free" LMS'. Hack Education http://www.hackeducation.com/2011/10/13/pearsons-free-lms/. [Last accessed 8th September 2014]

Watters, A. (2012) 'Don't Know Much about History (of Education)' http://hackeducation.com/2012/11/01/history-of-education-khan-academy/. [Last accessed 8th September 2014]

Watters, A. (2013) 'The Myth and the Millennialism of "Disruptive Innovation"' http://hackeducation.com/2013/05/24/disruptive-innovation/. [Last accessed 8th September 2014]

Weinberger, D. (2007) *Everything is miscellaneous: The power of the new digital disorder.* Macmillan.

The Wellcome Trust. (n.d.) Open access policy http://www.wellcome.ac.uk/About-us/Policy/Policy-and-position-statements/WTD002766.htm. [Last accessed 8th September 2014]

Weller, M. (2002) *Delivering Learning on the Net: the why, what & how of online education.* Kogan Page.

Weller, M. (2004) 'Models of Large Scale E-learning'. *JALN,* vol. 8, issue 4, December 2004.

Weller, M. (2007) 'First OU Facebook App' http://blog.edtechie.net/facebook/first-ou-facebo/. [Last accessed 8th September 2014]

Weller, M. (2011) 'Launching Meta EdTech Journal' http://blog.edtechie.net/publishing/launching-meta-edtech-journal/. [Last accessed 8th September 2014]

Weller, M. (2011) *The Digital Scholar: How Technology Is Transforming Scholarly Practice.* Basingstoke: Bloomsbury Academic.

Weller, M. (2012) 'The openness-creativity cycle in education: a perspective'. *Journal of Interactive Media in Education* http://jime.open.ac.uk/jime/article/view/2012-02. [Last accessed 8th September 2014]

Weller, M. and Robinson, L. (2002) 'Scaling up an online course to deal with 12,000 students'. *Education, Communication and Information*, 1(3), pp. 307–323.

Weller, M., Siemens, G., and Cormier, D. (2012) 'MOOCs' http://www.youtube.com/watch?v=l1G4SUblnbo. [Last accessed 8th September 2014]

Wild, J. (2012) 'OER Engagement Study: Promoting OER reuse among academics.' Research report from the SCORE funded project. http://www.open.ac.uk/score/files/score/file/OER%20Engagement%20Study%20Joanna%20Wild_full%20research%20report.pdf. [Last accessed 8th September 2014]

Wiley, D. (2004). *The Reusability Paradox.* Connexions http://cnx.org/contents/dad41956-c2b2-4e01-94b4-4a871783b021@19. [Last accessed 8th September 2014]

Wiley, D. (2007a) Open Education License Draft http://open
    content.org/blog/archives/355. [Last accessed 8th September
    2014]

Wiley, D. (2007b) 'On the Sustainability of Open Educational
    Resource Initiatives in Higher Education', *Paris, OECD.*
    https://www1.oecd.org/edu/ceri/38645447.pdf. [Last accessed
    8th September 2014]

Wiley, D. (2008) David Wiley: iSummit '08 Keynote Address http://
    vimeo.com/1796014. [Last accessed 8th September 2014]

Wiley, D. (2009) 'Dark Matter, Dark Reuse, and the Irrational
    Zeal of a Believer' http://opencontent.org/blog/archives/905.
    [Last accessed 8th September 2014]

Wiley, D. (2010) 'Openness as Catalyst for an Educational
    Reformation' *EDUCAUSE Review*, vol. 45, no. 4 (July/
    August 2010): 14–20 http://www.educause.edu/ero/article/
    openness-catalyst-educational-reformation. [Last accessed
    8th September 2014]

Wiley, D. (2011a) 'Openwashing – the new Greenwashing'
    http://opencontent.org/blog/archives/1934. [Last accessed 8th
    September 2014]

Wiley, D. (2011b) 'The $5 textbook' http://utahopentextbooks.
    org/2011/08/26/the-5-textbook/. [Last accessed 8th September
    2014]

Wiley, D. (2014) 'The Access Compromise and the 5th R'
    http://opencontent.org/blog/archives/3221. [Last   accessed
    8th September 2014]

Wiley, D. and Gurrell, S. (2009) 'A decade of development…',
    Open Learning: The Journal of Open, Distance and e-Learning,
    24:1, 11–21.

Wiley, D. and Green, C. (2012) 'Why openness in education?'
    In D. Oblinger (Ed.), *Game changers: Education and
    information technologies,* pp. 81–89. Educause.

Wiley, D., Levi Hilton III, J., Ellington, S., and Hall, T. (2012)
    'A Preliminary Examination of the Cost Savings and Learning
    Impacts of Using Open Textbooks in Middle and High

School Science Classes'. *The International Review of Research in Open and Distance Learning,* 13(3) http://www.irrodl.org/index.php/irrodl/article/view/1153/2256. [Last accessed 8th September 2014]

Williams, S. (2002) *Free as in Freedom: Richard Stallman's Crusade for Free Software.* O'Reilly Press. http://oreilly.com/openbook/freedom/. [Last accessed 8th September 2014]

Winn, J. (2012) 'Open education: from the freedom of things to the freedom of people'. *Towards teaching in public: reshaping the modern university.* London: Continuum.

Winn, J. (2013) 'A Cooperative University' http://josswinn.org/2013/11/a-co-operative-university/. [Last accessed 8th September 2014]

Wolfson, L. (2013) 'Venture Capital Needed for "Broken" U.S. Education, Thrun Says'. *Bloomberg Business Week,* June 18, 2013. http://www.businessweek.com/news/2013-06-18/venture-capital-needed-for-broken-u-dot-s-dot-education-thrun-says. [Last accessed 8th September 2014]

Worstall, T. (2013) 'What MOOCs Will Really Kill Is the Research University' *Forbes,* July 27. 2013 http://www.forbes.com/sites/timworstall/2013/07/27/what-moocs-will-really-kill-is-the-research-university/. [Last accessed 8th September 2014]

Young, J. (2012) 'Providers of Free MOOC's Now Charge Employers for Access to Student Data'. *The Chronicle of Higher Education* http://chronicle.com/article/Providers-of-Free-MOOCs-Now/136117/. [Last accessed 8th September 2014]

Yuan, L. and Powell, S. (2013) 'MOOCs and Open Education: Implications for Higher Education'. *CETIS White Paper* http://publications.cetis.ac.uk/2013/667. [Last accessed 8th September 2014]

Zevin, J. (2012) 'MOOCs as capital-biased technological change' http://themagnetisalwayson.com/moocs-as-capital-biased-technological-change/. [Last accessed 8th September 2014]

Zimmerman, N. (2014) 'Teen Posts Joke on Twitter, Internet Orders Her to Kill Herself'. *The Gawker* http://gawker.

com/teen-posts-joke-on-twitter-internet-orders-her-to-kill-1493156583. [Last accessed 8th September 2014]

Zuckerman, E. (2012) 'An idea worth at least 40 nanoKardashians of your attention' http://www.ethanzuckerman.com/blog/2012/05/02/an-idea-worth-at-least-40-nanokardashians-of-your-attention/. [Last accessed 8th September 2014]

Index

Lightning Source UK Ltd.
Milton Keynes UK
UKOW06f1119010315

247072UK00007B/14/P